Jean Vanier

Jean Vanier

Portrait of a Free Man

Anne-Sophie Constant

Translated by Allen Page

PLOUGH PUBLISHING HOUSE

Published by Plough Publishing House
Walden, New York
Robertsbridge, England
Elsmore, Australia
www.plough.com

Plough produces books, a quarterly magazine, and Plough.com to encourage people and help them put their faith into action. We believe Jesus can transform the world and that his teachings and example apply to all aspects of life. At the same time, we seek common ground with all people regardless of their creed.

Plough is the publishing house of the Bruderhof, an international Christian community. The Bruderhof is a fellowship of families and singles practicing radical discipleship in the spirit of the first church in Jerusalem (Acts 2 and 4). Members devote their entire lives to serving God, one another, and their neighbors, renouncing private property and sharing everything. To learn more about the Bruderhof's faith, history, and daily life, see Bruderhof.com. (Views expressed by Plough authors are their own and do not necessarily reflect the position of the Bruderhof.)

Originally published in French as *Jean Vanier, Portrait d'un Homme Libre*.
Copyright © 2014 by Éditions Albin Michel. All rights reserved.

Cover image: Stéphane Ouzounoff/CIRIC

ISBN: 978-0-87486-140-2
23 22 21 20 19   1 2 3 4 5 6 7

A catalog record for this book is available from the British Library.
Library of Congress Cataloging-in-Publication Data

Names: Constant, Anne-Sophie, author.
Title: Jean Vanier : protrait of a free man / Anne-Sophie Constant ;
    translated by Allen Page.
Other titles: Jean Vanier. English
Description: Walden, NY : Plough Publishing House, 2019.
Identifiers: LCCN 2018061619 (print) | LCCN 2019011224 (ebook) | ISBN
    9780874861242 (epub) | ISBN 9780874860207 (mobi) | ISBN 9780874861310 (
    pdf) | ISBN 9780874861402 (pbk. : alk. paper)
Subjects: LCSH: Vanier, Jean, 1928- | Arche (Association)
Classification: LCC BX4705.V34 (ebook) | LCC BX4705.V34 C6613 2019 (print) |
    DDC 267/.182092 [B] --dc23
LC record available at https://lccn.loc.gov/2018061619

Printed in the United States of America

To Jérôme

"There is but nostalgia in love.
When will I seize what has seized me?"
—Pierre Emmanuel, *Jacob*

"Anyone who listens to the word but does not do what it says is like
someone who looks at his face in a mirror and, after looking at
himself, goes away and immediately forgets what he looks like."
—The Letter of James

Contents

Introduction

IT'S A CRAZY STORY, or at least out of the ordinary. In August of 1964, a thirty-six-year-old Canadian who had been a naval officer, earned a PhD from the Catholic Institute of Paris, and taught ethics at the University of Toronto, took up residence in a little house in the village of Trosly, France, with two intellectually disabled people. The house, which he called L'Arche (the Ark), had neither water nor electricity. His plan? None. But he was convinced that he had to do it. He was touched by the silent cry of these men, who had been shut up in a gloomy, violent institution when he first met them.

A group quickly formed around the strange trio in L'Arche. Neighbors came to help, and friends joined them. Barely months after its creation, L'Arche became "a gathering of more than fifty people having links with the state, the church, and professionals."[1] Money came in, and structure and organization followed. Other L'Arche houses were soon receiving more residents from care homes. Women were welcomed into the community. Workshops were set up; a barn was turned into a church. In 1968, in Trosly, the communities consisted of seventy-three people; in 1970, one hundred and twelve; and in 1972, one hundred and twenty-six. L'Arche communities also sprang up in different contexts, societies, cultures, and religions. Communities arose in the north and south of France, Canada, India, England, Haiti, Honduras, and Australia. They were born in an organic way, without any strategy for expansion, most often following retreats or talks that Jean Vanier gave throughout the world. His words touched hearts. His example was contagious. It met an aching need.

IF THE STORY of the founding is surprising, even more surprising is the story of the founder. Here was a fervent Catholic who founded ecumenical and interreligious communities in which atheists felt at home, a sailor who settled on land, a philosopher who choose to live with people of limited intelligence. A child of privilege, he had danced with princesses, dined with politicians and philosophers, and circled the world twice. In 1964, his father was governor general of Canada and his mother was chancellor of the University of Ottawa. Why, then, did this talented young man chose to live in poverty with people who are so often and so tragically excluded and humiliated? Why did he, knowing nothing about physical or intellectual disabilities, commit to sharing his life with two unknown people? By what detours did he arrive at this new life, for which seemingly nothing in his training or background had prepared him?

The story of Jean Vanier is the story of a free man – a man who knew how to become himself, who knew how to free himself from restraints and prejudices; from intellectual, religious, or moral habits; from his epoch; from popular opinion. He was able to free himself from this great current in which we all swim, because he knew how to listen to his own inner voice – the conscience, which Saint Thomas Aquinas tells us is not just the ability to distinguish between good and evil, but a force that pulls us toward liberty, justice, and light. Jean Vanier followed this inner voice, aided by an extraordinary family and surprising encounters. He also experienced failures, renunciations, and disappointments.

Introduction

He dared – for a sailor this was no doubt normal – to cast off, abandon safety, and sail into the unknown. When he started L'Arche he did not have a precise map or a clear destination, but he had a compass, the same one he'd had since leaving the navy: "I want to live with Jesus." We are reminded of the rich young man in the Gospel, the one whom Jesus looked on and loved, and to whom he said: "One thing you lack. . . . Go, sell everything you have and give to the poor, and you will have treasure in heaven. Then come, follow me" (Mark 10:21).

JEAN VANIER HAS TRANSFORMED the lives of thousands of intellectually disabled people. He has rescued them from the streets, from institutions, and from houses where they were caged, and he has helped them find a more dignified life in L'Arche communities. In the many pilgrimages and meetings he has led, he has helped them find friends. Along with Faith and Light, another movement he inspired, he has wrested thousands of parents from their dreadful solitude by transforming how they understand the disabilities of their own children. Jean Vanier could tell a thousand stories of such parents, like the father in Burkina Faso who stood at the end of Jean's speech and thanked him by saying: "No one ever told us that our children were beautiful."

"No one ever told us that our children were beautiful!" Where we see only failure, impossibility, weakness, and suffering, Jean Vanier sees beauty, and knows how to open the eyes of others to see it too. Over the past fifty years, thousands have followed in his wake, making the same strange choice to live with people with intellectual disabilities, some for a few months, some for their whole lives. He has blazed a trail for others to follow, a trail that led to this little village of Trosly to which he has tied his destiny, as have so many others.

Yet there is something about Jean Vanier that evades description. I have rubbed shoulders with him for many years, have listened to him, read his writings, and written many pages about him – despite all this, he remains an enigma. Who is this man? To answer these questions, I asked Jean if I could write his biography, interviewing him – and his friends – in the process.

Jean agreed. He answered all my questions graciously, sparing neither time nor energy. He was a bit worried that I would embellish his portrait, set him on a pedestal. Yes, he recognizes that the story is surprising. Himself? Of that he is less sure.

But I am sure that Jean Vanier has become one of the great figures of our time. He has received prizes and distinctions and already has his place in heaven, since there is an asteroid named after him! His work on behalf of disabled people is undeniable, but it would be wrong to think that his message only applies to them. He is concerned about each one of us and our society, with the fragility and beauty of humanity, and the possibility of unity. He is a messenger of peace. He is a man at peace, a free man.

Anne-Sophie Constant

I

Child of War

WHEN JEAN VANIER CALLS himself a child of war, he is thinking of World War II. But the story opens earlier, against the backdrop of tragedy that was World War I. Indeed, his whole early childhood unfolded in the shadow of the Great War of 1914 to 1918. That war determined his father's career, led to his parents' marriage, and shaped a family attitude in the face of adversity and the misfortune of others. The battlefields were far from Montreal, so Georges Vanier could have considered the European drama none of his concern. Yet he voluntarily enlisted in the only battalion of French Canadians, the renowned 22nd. This would determine the course of his whole life. He would become a hero admired by many, including his son Jean.

In 1998, when *Maclean's* drew up a list of the hundred most important Canadians of all time, Georges Vanier was first on the list. "A man of courage and sacrifice, in war as in peace," the magazine read, adding that he had been "a moral compass for Canada, a man of unquestioned integrity and honor." Jean's mother, Pauline, had a generosity, courage, ardent faith, and commitment to the poor that made her an exceptional personality too. Though his life would take a different turn, Jean acknowledges how instrumental his parents were in his formation.

It wasn't always easy, however. Because he was the child of a diplomat, his parents were often absent. The family moved frequently, so he was knocked about between Switzerland, England, France, and Canada. Caught between cultures and between two languages and two mothers – his mother and his beloved nanny – he wasn't able to put down roots and feel at home.

Jean Vanier would finally find his home with L'Arche. But strangely enough, as he aged, he associated this home, where he had been able to rediscover the child within himself, with being in the mud. "I finally have my feet in the mud," he wrote in 2011. "Life at L'Arche transformed me, and I finally found a place where I could commit myself – a commitment that gave me life. With my feet in the mud, and with constant difficulties, L'Arche has grown."[1] He repeated this unusual expression in various talks and writings. What is this mud in which one can find life, this mud where blood and dirt mingle? Given his family history, one is reminded of the mud in the trenches of World War I, where his father fought and distinguished himself.

The Crucible of War

WHEN JEAN FRANÇOIS ANTOINE was born in Geneva on September 10, 1928, his father, General Georges Philias Vanier, was the Canadian military representative to the League of Nations. He did things backward: first war, then the Royal Canadian Military College, and finally international peacemaking.

The war of 1914–18 had been a crucible in which the unlikely destiny of Georges Vanier was forged. He was a deeply religious man. Educated by the Jesuits, he considered the priesthood, but eventually recognized it was not the path he should follow. A boxing and hockey enthusiast and dabbler in art and poetry, he had never shown the least interest in a military career. As soon as war was declared, however, he did not hesitate to leave his career as a lawyer and his comfortable life in Montreal behind. The military offered him a way to serve and commit himself to a higher cause. Such a reaction among Canadians – particularly French Canadians – was not very widespread. Because of a lack of volunteers to feed the battlefields of Europe, a compulsory draft was instated in 1917, and 96 percent of the draftees requested exemption.

After his military training, the twenty-seven-year-old traveled to England before disembarking at Le Havre on September 20, 1915, and heading for the Ypres region – a particularly violent combat zone. Surrounded by the crater-scarred landscape of mud, snow, and icy wind, Georges and his fellow soldiers withstood artillery shells and bombs, entombed day and night in the narrow guts of the trenches. On January 2, 1916, Georges Vanier commanded a little detachment of volunteers who, crawling at night, penetrated the enemy barbed wire and blew up a German machine gun post that was spraying shells on the Canadian lines.

The *Montreal Press* reported the exploit, but almost no mention of it appeared in the letters of the young lieutenant. Instead, his correspondence described the dismal landscape and incessant bombings with an air of detachment that was almost comic. On a more serious note, his correspondence manifested his concern for his family. He encouraged his younger brother Anthony in his studies, rejoiced at the marriage of his sister Eva, and teased his youngest sister, Frances. Above all, he was careful not to cause anyone worry.

A scrupulous and upright man, Georges discovered that he had a natural gift for exercising authority. He was promoted to captain, and was the first in his regiment to be decorated with the coveted Military Cross, which was only awarded for heroic armed deeds in the face of the enemy. People loved him because of his respect for others, his great courtesy, and his sense of service.

As company commander on the front lines, Georges was wounded for the first time in June 1916 in the Ypres Salient. He was treated in French Flanders, at the Mont des Cats monastery, which had been converted into a field hospital, and was repatriated to England. He refused an offer to go back to Canada and returned to combat three months later.

Georges took part in all the great battles in which Canadians fought: Vimy, Hill 70, Passchendaele, and, finally, Chérisy – a horrendous slaughter.

Chérisy

THE WEATHER WAS BEAUTIFUL on the twenty-seventh of August, 1918, when the 22nd launched an assault on what historians say was the most dangerous point of the most dangerous sector of the Hindenburg Line. The next evening, in a field of desolation and ruin, only thirty-seven out of seven hundred soldiers had survived. All the officers were either killed or seriously wounded. Georges Vanier, who took command when a major was killed during the assault, was wounded on August 28. He underwent an emergency leg amputation at the Boulogne Hospital and was evacuated to London. On November 11, he had to undergo a second amputation that cut the femur a little higher. He was taken to the operating room to the sound of the cannons welcoming the Armistice.

It was many long months before he could stand. He suffered through a wooden leg, physical rehabilitation, and phantom pain, but all he mentioned in letters to his family was his favorable progress. He waited three months before telling his mother about the amputation, and never mentioned the appalling hemorrhage that nearly killed him, nor the extent of his sufferings, hinted at only in his personal diary.

Because of his operation on Armistice Day, he did not return to Canada with the rest of the 22nd Battalion. He returned alone because he wanted to return on his feet. The war was etched into him. And yet, as far as we know, he was not bitter. We might dare think, even, that his wounds led to a more intimate encounter with God. Like Jacob, after his night of struggle at the ford of Jabbok, he limped, wounded by the angel. Then, against all expectations, and to the great astonishment of all, especially the inspector general of the armed forces, the young man, now discharged and declared unfit for service, did not return to his career as a lawyer, but requested to become a career officer.

He related the scene in his correspondence with his characteristic mixture of modesty and comedy. "General Currie started laughing, gently, but he laughed. He said to me, 'You have lost a leg.' I answered, 'I know that, but don't you need men with heads as much as you need men with legs?' . . . I left without much hope. We had laughed together, knowing (at least that was my impression) that it was impossible, but three weeks later I found myself second in command of the regiment."[2]

After his marriage to Pauline Archer in 1921, the second commander of the Royal 22nd Regiment attended the Royal Canadian Military College in Kingston, Ontario, where the young couple spent their first months of married life. They then moved on to Ottawa, where Georges had just been named aide-de-camp to the new governor general. They left for England together in January 1922, because the brilliant officer had just been appointed to Staff College of Camberley, in Surrey, about thirty miles from London. Strategy, high command, army organization, geopolitics, and two years of high-level training shaped his career as an officer, then as a diplomat.

JEAN VANIER'S FATHER didn't like to talk about himself, nor about the war. With a great gentleness in his eyes, he maintained a certain distance from the painful events in his memory. The children did not ask how he got his wound. However, they could not ignore it. They saw their father climbing steps one by one, leaning on a cane. They listened as he told funny stories about one-legged men – his specialty. "We never heard him complain," Jean Vanier wrote in 1967. "He even knew how to laugh at the reason for his fatigue: the loss of his leg. Instead of making a drama out of it to draw sympathy to himself, he liked to make jokes about his hinged leg. When we were children, he would put us on his knee and give us a pin, saying, 'Now you're going to see how stoic I am.' He told us to stick the pin in his leg. Sometimes also, when we were taking a walk, he would strike his leg with his cane, saying, 'You see how hard my leg is.'"[3]

When Jean was born there were already three children: Thérèse, born in England in 1923, and Georges and Bernard, born in Canada in 1925 and 1927. Little Michel, the youngest, was born in 1941, also in Canada. The children were familiar with the name Chérisy. Surprisingly, the couple named their first child Thérèse Marie Chérisy, as though the suffering, heartbreak, and terror of the war were mixed up with their union and the creation of new life. From the beginning, the mystery of suffering belonged to their story.

Chérisy, at the heart of their story, was also the cause of their meeting. The commander in chief of Georges's battalion, Brigadier-General Thomas-Louis Tremblay, introduced him to Pauline Archer one beautiful afternoon in September, while they were having tea in the Ritz Hotel in Montreal.

"She Is the Better Half"

PAULINE ARCHER WAS TWENTY-ONE when she met Georges Vanier in 1920. He was ten years her senior. She was very thin and almost six feet tall. She had, in fact, served as a model for the sculptor Alfred Laliberté, representing Civilization in a monument dedicated to Jacques Cartier. Under a crown of black hair, she had very blue eyes and a dazzling smile.

Georges and Pauline were not exactly from the same world. Georges's father was a self-made man. Employed by an Irish grocer, whose daughter he married, he rapidly expanded the business and made a fortune, although he had practically no education. Pauline's mother, Thérèse d'Irumberry de Salaberry, traced her ancestry back to the kings of Navarre. She received spiritual direction from

Almire Pichon, the Jesuit father who was a friend of the Martin family in Lisieux and had been the spiritual director of the future saint, Thérèse Martin herself. Pauline's father, Charles Archer, was a Quebec Supreme Court judge. He studied at the prestigious Laval University, as did his future son-in-law, and enjoyed a vast fortune, which was built by his forebears in the mining and construction industries.

As a child, Pauline lacked nothing that riches and social standing could offer. She was perfectly bilingual, learned Italian and Spanish as well, played the piano, and knew how to behave properly. She was educated at a convent, until ill health forced her to leave, whereupon a McGill University professor taught her literature. Because her studies were interrupted, she was left with somewhat of a complex. She could be exuberant and sure of herself, but also fragile and depressive.

She was a passionate soul, animated by a deep faith. She also considered a possible religious vocation, but decided against it. Like Georges, she looked for ways to serve and to find her place in the world. The war opened a crack in her otherwise well-ordered world. She signed up for a program to support soldiers and, as a war sponsor, corresponded with two Belgian officers. When she learned that the Red Cross was looking for nurses, she went to work in the hospital among wounded repatriated soldiers – without informing her mother. She joined in the festivities that marked the return of the 22nd Battalion, making the acquaintance of Thomas Trembley, who later introduced her to her future husband.

GEORGES VANIER WAS DAZZLED when Trembley introduced Pauline, and he invited her to dinner the very next day. They talked about France, war, and topography. Very soon, in fact, she was to embark on a long trip to France, where she would tour the battlefields. She was also to meet an officer with whom she had exchanged letters that had become more and more affectionate. Before departing, she waited in vain for a bouquet that she felt she had every right to expect – and that Georges really had sent. Unfortunately, it had been mistakenly delivered to another ship. So she visited the famous places of the Canadian war in France, got engaged to the handsome officer, broke off the engagement, and returned to Canada.

With the help of another regimental friend she got back in touch with Georges, who invited her to Quebec. Several days into a courtship during which they spoke more about philosophy and literature than about love, he asked her to marry him, and she accepted. She wished to marry on August 28, 1921, the anniversary of the day Georges was wounded. However, nothing would have been ready by that date, and so they were married on September 29.

The couple was passionately in love. Later Pauline said, "My life had been fulfilled and I was showered with gifts from God. I married Georges Vanier and that was the greatest of the gifts."[4] They shared the same faith and the same outlook on life. They chose to serve together, too. She was to accompany him everywhere, even if she had to leave Michel, her youngest son, in the care of her mother. And Georges always leaned on her, even while supporting her. She spent herself without reserve for the sake of the wounded, refugees, and children, and she accomplished noteworthy tasks in post-war France and Canada. As her husband wrote in 1961: "She overtook me in fulfilling the shared tasks and duties that fell to us. She is the better half of the team!"[5]

Nanny Thompson

IN 1931, WHEN JEAN was still a young boy, Georges Vanier was appointed to the Canadian High Commission in London. Life was peaceful in the London home, although the financial crisis that began the Great Depression depleted the family fortune. Georges Vanier hadn't made the best investments, and the family experienced financial difficulties that forced them to move to a smaller house. When Father came home, he would let out a little whistle to signal his presence, and the children would come downstairs to greet him. Mother made them recite their prayers each morning and evening, and the whole family went to Mass on Sunday.

Like the children of good English families of the time, Jean and his siblings were raised by nannies. They lived in the nursery and saw their parents briefly in the evening before they left for various receptions that embassy life required. Isabel Thompson, Jean's nanny, was greatly loved by the family. Nanny Thompson was hired when Thérèse was born and didn't leave the Vanier home until Jean went to boarding school in 1937. He owes the nickname "Jock" to her (Jean was too difficult for a Scottish person to pronounce). More than anyone, it was she who raised him, and whenever he recalls his childhood he always speaks of her with a tender smile. "She saved me," he says. "I loved her more than I loved my mother."[6]

Pauline Vanier was loving but rather distant with her children. Already easily anxious and overwhelmed by her role as a mother, she fell into a deep depression after the birth of her fourth child. The pregnancy had been difficult, and she was bedridden for a long time. She also found it difficult to recover from the shock of a fire in their country home, in which they all nearly perished. It's hard to say what else troubled her, but she was sick for three years.

Whenever Jean talks about his mother – and he doesn't do so very willingly – he describes someone who was both exuberant and depressive, someone who oscillated rapidly from despondency to expressions of overwhelming tenderness. He was the youngest child for a long time, and for three years she was either emotionally absent or possessive. Recalling memories of childhood wounds, Jean once wrote, "Some people have had depressive or possessive mothers who did everything to keep them from growing up, so that they would remain 'little' children who were bound to them."[7] Was he talking about their relationship? Curiously, he also maintains that she had great spiritual strength and was a woman with an admirable faith, sure of God's love for her and for every person.

Jean was a happy child – quick-tempered, perhaps, but disciplined. He himself says that he was a good boy who had neither distinctive qualities nor brilliant talents. He followed his brothers to the little private neighborhood school, and he would later follow them to the Jesuit college of St. John. He was, however, less hearty than they, and often sick. He also had his head in the clouds and was a bit restless, but he learned easily. He was especially close to his brother Bernard, who was only a year older. The two would plot against their elder siblings, who frightened them a little. As Bernard said, "They were stronger, it's true, but they were separate . . . while we two were together!"

Jean enjoyed a loving family, a tender nanny, and a comfortable home. But the next war was about to change all that.

"I Remember the Wailing"

GEORGES VANIER WAS APPOINTED Canadian ambassador to France in January 1939.[8] The children stayed in England to finish their school year, and the family came together for vacations in Varangeville, on the coast of Normandy. Jean remembers the vacations as happy times. The weather was beautiful; Father played tennis, and the children went to the beach. During delicious meals at the Hôtel de la Terrasse, each person could select his or her favorite cheese – the maître d'hôtel was careful to remember that Jean's favorite was Pont l'Eveque. Jean also remembers when war was declared and how it spread throughout the world in a game of alliances and empires. At 11 o'clock on the third of September, the United Kingdom declared war on Germany. France, Australia, and New Zealand followed at five that evening. On Jean's eleventh birthday, the tenth of September, it was Canada's turn to declare war.

Fearful of bombings and not knowing what would happen next, the family settled in Baillou Castle, home of the Marquis of Cortavel, while Georges returned to his post in Paris. The ambassador also made round trips between Paris and Baillou, with Pauline sometimes accompanying him. Thérèse, who had finished her secondary studies, stayed at the castle with Jean, who was sick, while his brothers continued their studies at the Jesuit college in Saint-Calais. Life in the castle was gloomy without his sidekick Bernard.

THE FAMILY RETURNED to Paris in April of 1940. But in May of 1940, Germany invaded Belgium as well as France, whose roads were soon clogged with masses of refugees. Between May 15 and June 10, six million people fled the combat. Among them were Jean and his family. They left Paris, seven people crammed into an embassy car. Georges remained, but Pauline's mother, Thérèse de Salaberry, who had been living with them since her husband died in 1934, came along. The journey was difficult, and gasoline was scarce. The car advanced by inches, bumper to bumper, through a monstrous traffic jam. Their car passed thousands of out-of-gas vehicles along the roadside. People on foot pulled carts or walked along with farm animals. Air raid alarms forced everyone to travel with their headlights extinguished, which heightened anxiety. What Jean remembers, however, was not so much his own fear as that of other people – "these hundreds of thousands of frightened people who were fleeing the oppressor."[9] They finally arrived at Chitenay, a village about nine miles from Blois, where they were welcomed into the home of a cousin.

On June 14, the French government and the ambassadors withdrew from Tours and headed for Bordeaux ahead of the advancing German troops. At the same time, the Vaniers took to the highway. They met Georges in Margaux and traveled together to Cantenac, a village near the port of Verdon-sur-Mer, where they waited to board a ship along with the Canadian legation. The mayor's office provided lodging for them in an improvised camp, and the family spread out mattresses and blankets on the ground for lack of anything better. Finally, on June 17, they boarded an English destroyer that transported them to the *Nariva*, an Argentinian cargo ship that had been diverted from its route to England to pick up refugees.

They lacked water and food, and were squeezed six to a cabin. Jean shared a berth with his grandmother. He said, with humor, that she "had my socks up her nose." The ship had to tack back and forth between mines in its attempt to escape the German submarines. It made a huge detour, and took four days to arrive at Milford Haven in Wales. In spite of feeling the invisible presence of the enemy and hearing the muffled thudding of bombs as they left the Bay of Biscay, this was an exciting adventure for the little boy. Yet a terrifying image was etched in his mind one evening, and the adventure turned into a very painful event.

Jean recalls the *Nariva*'s encounter with an enormous ferry carrying hundreds of howling people. "They wanted to board our vessel, but the captain refused. There were already too many people. How many were we on board? Two hundred, three hundred, perhaps five hundred on a ship that was not equipped for that many people. There was not enough water or food. I remember the wailing when they saw our ship turn away. We left. And it was awful. . . . We later became friends with one of the officers, and he told us that the captain of the ferry, upon arriving at his destination, had committed suicide."[10]

THE VANIER FAMILY ARRIVED in London after a final journey by train. At the beginning of July, the children and their grandmother boarded the *Batory*, a Polish liner headed for Canada. Georges Vanier remained behind, as did Pauline, who did not want to be separated from her husband. The voyage on the liner was comfortable, but worrisome, since German submarines were prowling the Atlantic. One day in the dining room, where there was a radio, the children were listening to German propaganda that was broadcast in English with an authentic British accent, and learned that their ship had just been sunk!

In London, Georges Vanier was fighting for Allied recognition of General de Gaulle and the Free French. Pauline, who was involved in the Red Cross, was visiting wounded French soldiers in the hospital. In letters to her children, she told them what she was doing and what London was like under the bombing. Neither she nor her husband wanted to return to Canada, feeling that their place was in Europe while it was at war. But when the Canadian government appointed Georges Vanier to the Joint US–Canadian Defense Commission, they finally returned to Montreal in October 1940.

The reunited family settled in an apartment, and life began again. The children attended Loyola College, which had been their father's school. They were sheltered but had not escaped the war. "Of course we talked about the war, and about heroism, and often about heroes," Jean Vanier recounts. His father cast the conflict in universal and religious terms: "It was not an ordinary war between people. It was a war in which the forces of materialism and evil confronted those of the spirit."[11] Georges Vanier spoke, too, about the vital duty to aid the victims of war: "In Europe, thousands of souls in distress are crying out to heaven. These are the disinherited, the oppressed, those under the scourge of Hitler. They are calling us to help them. Like Deblois, I cry out, 'We can't let them die alone.'" This call echoed in the conscience of young Jean, who still recalled those refugees turned away by the *Nariva*.

The Dartmouth Choice

TIME PASSED: house, school, daily Mass, play. The child who was fragile and who easily fell sick gained strength. And then one day, Jean turned thirteen. As he looks back today – though it is hard to believe – he describes himself as rather mediocre, average in school and sports, lacking personality and assertion. But this thirteen-year-old had a surprising idea, his first truly personal wish. He wanted to join the navy and enroll in a military school in England, the Royal Naval College in Dartmouth.

Maybe the idea was not so surprising. It was 1942, and Jean knew he could not remain a spectator in the face of global suffering. The image of the refugees on the ferry still haunted him. His sister Thérèse, now nineteen, had joined the Canadian Army the year before. Looking back, Jean freely recognizes that he was probably trying to follow in the footsteps of his heroic father. It's also easy to imagine – he himself suggests it – that he might have wanted to distinguish himself from his brothers who were so brilliant in school, or to escape from a mother whose love was a bit stifling. His brother Bernard, who had always been his friend and accomplice, thought later that it was a movie about navy cadets that prompted this strange urge.

THAT IS ALL POSSIBLE, but it doesn't explain everything, for the most surprising thing was not the idea itself, but the force of it: Jean was absolutely convinced that this was what he should do. "I don't know why I was so certain," he says. "This was the first time I had had a desire, a desire that came from me, and that desire . . . prodded me to leave my family and go to a Protestant military college. . . . What prods people? What prodded me? I have asked myself that question for years. I think it's the personal conscience that finally sweeps us up and carries us away. I can say that I was swept up."[12]

The determined youth made inquiries and assembled the documents required for enrollment in Dartmouth. He wrote to his father and asked to meet him in his office at military headquarters. His father listened to him and tried to dissuade him, pointing out the dangers of the undertaking. Jean was only thirteen. Europe was at war, and one out of every five ships in the Atlantic was being sunk. He was Canadian, and a Catholic. His family would be far away. If he was attracted to the navy, he could join the Vancouver Naval School when he turned seventeen. And then his father asked him why he wanted to sign up. Jean no longer remembers what he answered, but he has never forgotten his father's response. Georges not only accepted but added: "I trust you. If you think you have to do it, then do it."

The incomprehensible character of his father's consent still strikes Jean many years later. "It would have been so easy to refuse, to say no. I would have accepted; I would have understood and would not have revolted. But something would have been shattered in me. I would have been deeply wounded. His confidence in me gave me confidence in myself, confidence in my intuitions. For a second time he gave me life."[13]

What could Georges Vanier have seen in Jean that convinced him to let the boy go? Perhaps he intuited Jean's special calling, as is evidenced by what he tearfully told his wife when he announced the news: "You know, we mustn't clip the child's wings. We don't know what he might become later." Georges's Christian faith was also marked by the conviction that we are not created for ourselves alone: we must find the meaning of our existence by discerning a God-given mission for which we are accountable to God. In dealing with others, Jean would remember this lesson he had received on freedom, and the importance of freely following God's call above all else.

Learning to Be Different

GEORGES VANIER ACCOMPANIED JEAN by train all the way to Halifax, where the child boarded a troop transport, a convoy of twenty vessels escorted by destroyers. He was the only one of his age on board. No one escorted him, nor did anyone especially take charge of him. He had a private cabin, but dined with the officers. By way of distraction, he noted the number of depth charges launched by the ships responsible for their protection. He still remembers the deadened sound of the underwater explosions and the gushing of the foam. Fireworks from below signaled the proximity of enemy submarines prowling somewhere in the depths.

He disembarked at Liverpool, still alone, and took a train to London. His sister was supposed to meet him, but no one was at the station! The telegram announcing his arrival must have been lost. He hailed a taxi and traveled across the city to the address where Thérèse was lodging. Nobody answered when he rang the doorbell. Exhausted, he lay down on the landing and promptly fell asleep. He went by himself to order his uniforms at the tailor, then took the train to Dartmouth, in the south of England, where the Royal Naval College was located.

Jean arrived at the end of May 1942. He was late, since the semester had begun in April. "Everyone was there before me," he recalls. "What strikes me today is that I was not homesick in the least. No tears, no regrets, at least as far as I can remember. I was swept up into a sort of whirlwind, and I did what was necessary."[14] During adolescence, that complicated age when young people have such a desire to blend in, Jean Vanier seemed to accept his new surroundings with ease, in spite of the fact that he stood out. He showed up in street clothes after the school year had already begun, while all the cadets were in uniform; he was much taller than most of his fellow students; he was a Canadian among Englishmen; he was a Catholic among Anglicans. Yet he was a good comrade, and popular.

Jean never doubted his religion and practiced it as much as he could. When he left his family, he was uprooted from a deeply Catholic milieu with daily Mass and prayers. The religious atmosphere at Dartmouth was less pronounced, and the cadets were mostly Anglican and Protestant. During daily prayers a strange routine took place. As the five hundred students were assembled at attention on the parade field, a voice called, "Catholics, break ranks!" The few Catholics advanced a step, then trotted away to recite a Hail Mary behind a suitable hedge, while the others struck up an Our Father. On Sunday, a bus took them to Mass, and once a month a chaplain came for religious education.

Jean still laughs about the absurd prayer segregation, but he feels shocked that no one there ever encouraged him to read the Gospels. Instead, the chaplain offered the young boy a work of Christian apologetics. He took what was offered and, without much interest, dutifully read proofs of the existence of God. "Crazy, it was crazy!" he exclaims. "I read, but I didn't realize who God was. These days I would be given the Gospels to read!"[15] He also frequently visited the Anglican chaplain and began a dialog that continued by correspondence after he left the school. Religion, both his own and that of others, interested him, and he showed himself to be open to differing facets of the same quest to know God. He sought to understand others' paths, without ever doubting his own faith.

Preparing for War

JEAN'S TRAINING AT THE NAVAL COLLEGE lasted three years. It consisted of general studies (mathematics, language, English culture, history, and naval history), lots of sports, and training in navigation. The cadets diligently exercised on the Dart River. They learned how to equip a ship, handle a sailboat, and navigate by rowing. On land, they always moved from one place to another at a jog. They were being prepared for war. Indeed, war came to find them: the school was bombed and its facilities destroyed in September of 1942 at precisely eleven o'clock, the same day the students were supposed to have returned to school, and at the exact hour when they should have been at parade. However, the school was empty. For unknown reasons, the return to school had been postponed several days. Studies continued in Bristol several weeks later, the time it took the navy to figure out a contingency plan for the semester. Later, the school and its five hundred students moved to Chester, near Liverpool. Jean was a good student. He received good grades and was soon named "cadet captain," becoming one of the few student leaders.

The cadets listened intently to the radio, read the newspapers, and received news about the conflict from their superiors. The 1944 Allied landing at Normandy excited them, as did the progress of the Allied troops. But to the accounts of heroism were soon added unbearable images and stories that would haunt the young Vanier for a long time.

In the spring of 1945, Jean accompanied his mother to the Gare d'Orsay in Paris to welcome deportees who had been rescued from Buchenwald, Dachau, and Bergen-Belsen concentration camps. "I remember those men and women," he wrote in 1993, "who were still in their white-and-blue-striped uniforms. They were mere skeletons upon their arrival, and their faces were tortured with fear and anguish. What human beings are capable of inflicting on others, when driven by hate and the desire to crush their fellow men and women, can rise to unspeakable heights."[16] They learned that Joseph, the embassy chauffeur who had driven them along the French roads in 1940 during their exodus, had been deported. The mother of Georges's secretary died in Ravensbrück and her father in Buchenwald. In April, barely ten days after the camp's liberation, Georges Vanier went to Buchenwald. His eyewitness report described the atrocities. Shortly thereafter, the war was over. "The atomic bombs that were dropped in August 1945 on Hiroshima and Nagasaki caused unbearable suffering. In an instant, they killed, mutilated, and irradiated tens of thousands of people," Jean Vanier would later write in his book *A Door of Hope*.

WHEN THE CADETS were finally ready to take part in the conflict, the war had been over for four months. In December 1945, seventeen-year-old midshipman Jean Vanier left the Dartmouth Royal Naval College. According to his end-of-studies evaluation, he was "a very promising young officer, extremely open and cheerful, yet serious and professional when in a position of responsibility, who seemed to be a natural leader with considerable influence."[17] He was slated to meet the *Frobisher*, a training ship of the Royal Navy. Fifty cadets boarded the ship to complete their navigation training. They were finally on the ocean, and heading for new lands far from the tranquil currents of the Dart River. At the time, Jean Vanier didn't know that he would also acquire a different training during these years, and that he would reach a completely different shore.

2

Officer

WHEN JEAN VANIER REFLECTS upon the story of his life today, he can see, emerging from the visible events, signs of an invisible story. Seventy years after joining the navy, Jean believes his choice brought about meaningful events, whose significance had been hidden at the time. First of all, there was the trust that his father showed him when he allowed him to leave: "My father freed me," he wrote in 2009. That moment had been a rite of passage. "I could be myself, leave the family, follow a nonconformist path. I could risk living."[1] The time he spent at the college, as well as his years in the navy, were also essential to his development. Strange though it may seem, these stages in his career prepared him for his work with the intellectually disabled.

"I am convinced," he says today, "that my joining the navy was an act of God. More and more, I feel that I was carried, directed. I did not have a plan, but a certainty. Where did that certainty come from? That is a mystery, but it's there. I'm convinced that I had been prepared, fashioned to receive grace and discover my path and mission. Yes, I truly believe that I was thus prepared for a special mission. Each person has a specific mission, whether hidden or visible, but some have a special mission. For me, L'Arche has been that mission. A gift. A gift from God."

"If I had stayed in Canada, with my disposition, everything would have turned out differently. I would have remained docile instead of breaking ranks. I would have had a more intellectual training. I would have studied philosophy and theology with the Jesuits. I would have been more scholarly, but my understanding of faith, the church, and God would have been more theoretical. I would then have gone to the Sorbonne to finish my studies and would no doubt have become a priest. But my life took a completely different course, more adventurous and less according to the norm. My naval training away from home in England, among Anglicans, played an essential role. Not knowing what kinds of thought and action were acceptable, not knowing what was sound doctrine . . . I had more freedom."[2]

At an age when most adolescents were seeking meaning in their lives, Jean found meaning in his commitment to the navy. He was constantly working toward a goal greater than himself. On a spiritual level, his eight years in the navy were also a time to move beyond the more traditional streams of the church, as they existed in Canada at the time. On a physical level, he grew strong and learned about courage and endurance. He also trained to take command. He knew how to quickly recognize a right course of action and how to lead men in his wake. His experience as cadet captain and his years of service also taught him about solidarity and team spirit.

Aboard the Frobisher and the Vanguard

THE HMS *FROBISHER* WEIGHED ANCHOR in January 1946 for its first long voyage. It left for the Antilles, stopping first in Jamaica, where the beginnings of a revolution were shaking the country. The sailors were outfitted for war: helmets, rifles, and even bayonets. The British Empire needed to show force. During the voyage things calmed down, so once again, war evaded the young sailors. It was a peaceful training craft that entered Montego Bay, where they were met with the usual fanfare and ceremonies. Like the *Jeanne-d'Arc* in France, this training ship was also an ambassadorial vessel. The governor, local authorities, and British citizens held a reception for the young men.

Life was harsher in between port calls. The sailors worked on the ship from the engine room to the bridge. Rising at five in the morning, they worked in their bare feet, polishing the deck with a brush, greasing the motors, and checking fluid levels. As they used to say: "If it doesn't move, paint it white; if it moves, salute it!" They stood watches and even endured several storms.

Jean the midshipman had discovered life at sea, with its mix of demands and esprit-de-corps, of tradition and rites, of overcrowding and solitude. Jean felt a solid deck beneath his feet, but underneath the reassuring panting of the engine, there was always the muffled and unsettling sound of the immense sea. The elements could be mastered, but at any moment the forces of nature could make one feel one's own fragility. It was no accident that Jean Vanier had chosen a life on the sea in the navy rather than on the land in the army.

Four months later, the *Frobisher* returned to Great Britain. After some weeks of vacation – just enough time to rediscover a bed after sleeping in a hammock – the ship set off again, in the direction of Sweden, Denmark, and Norway. Having navigated the seas to the south, they were heading north for four months. Then, sufficiently hardened to maritime life, they would receive their first assignments as officers.

MIDSHIPMEN JEAN VANIER and Geoffrey Upfill-Brown were assigned to the prestigious HMS *Vanguard*. It was, in fact, on the *Vanguard* that King George VI, Queen Elizabeth, and their two daughters, Elizabeth and Margaret, were to travel on their official visit to South Africa. It was not by chance that these two officers were chosen for such a mission. Jean Vanier's qualities of seriousness, commitment, rigor, and leadership had been appreciated aboard the *Frobisher*. Of course, the name Vanier was also well-known. Jean's superiors may have forgotten that King George V himself had decorated Georges Vanier with the Military Cross in 1916 and the Distinguished Service Order in 1918, or that this same Georges Vanier had represented his country during the coronation ceremony of George VI in 1936, but surely everyone knew that this midshipman was the son of the Canadian ambassador to France.

In February 1947, Jean and Geoffrey cast off on the *Vanguard* with the royal family. In addition to his navigation tasks and the various services incumbent on an officer, Jean received a special task. Along with one of his comrades, he was charged with editing a newspaper that the king could read at breakfast. The budding young writers had the privilege of rising a little later than the other officers, but starting at ten in the evening they met in the radio room to listen to the world news. They selected, edited, and laid out the text, then produced a printed newspaper. They often went to bed quite late.

Jean was also recruited to provide distractions for the royal guests, in particular the princesses. Games, concerts, and plays filled the afternoons, and the midshipmen were often called upon in turn to take tea with the young ladies. This was the first official voyage for Elizabeth. She celebrated her twenty-first birthday in Durban and, at a grand ball that ended the festivities, Jean Vanier was appointed dance partner to Elizabeth's younger sister, Margaret. "She was light, cheerful, and a perfect dancer," he recalls. "As for me, I felt clumsy. I didn't know what to say, and I admit I didn't dance very well."

Did the glamor of the voyage distract the nineteen-year-old Jean Vanier? Was he charmed by the princesses? Did he meet other young women? Did he dream of love or marriage? "No," he says simply, "I didn't think about it. I was focused on what I was doing, on my assignment. The evenings, dinners, and mundane discussions bored me, and when, upon our arrival in port, my comrades went dancing, I looked for a church. And then, afterward, when I left the navy," he adds, "it was to become a priest, and that choice included celibacy."³

At L'Arche, Jean and numerous assistants would choose a life consecrated to celibacy, since people with intellectual disabilities often live celibately without a choice. In his 1984 book *Man and Woman God Made Them*, which he revised in 2009, Jean Vanier analyzes the origin and significance of the search for love that affects all of us. He shows how community relationships based on trust, respect, recognition, and tenderness can partially satisfy emotional demands. But he also notes that only God can fulfill the great desire of each person to be loved beyond measure. He writes that "celibacy for the sake of the kingdom" is a calling from Jesus, "the most excellent mediator, who, in the recesses of our hearts, says: 'Fear not, I love you. You are precious in my sight, you can live. Advance along the path of life to become, in your turn, a mediator who reveals to others that they are forgiven and loved.'"⁴

In any event, in 1947, amid the splendor of the *Vanguard* and the mist of the ocean spray, Jean Vanier seemed a long way from a calling to the priesthood, or even regular religious practice.

A Brush with Death

THE *VANGUARD* RETURNED to port in May, and the young officer was assigned to a battleship in Plymouth. While serving on the battleship, Jean had a near-death experience. He wrote in 2011, "I remember my first encounter with death – *my* death. But it did not come!"

Jean was in command of a landing craft that transported sailors from the battleship, anchored out at sea, to the shore. The craft was attached to a floating anchor that had to be detached. One day, the sea was rough and the wind violent. The landing craft pulled away from the side of the ship, preventing the sailors from boarding. Jean and his colleague were not able to pull the craft closer. The young officer hooked one arm on the rope ladder and the other to the rigging, trying to pull it in. He pulled and pulled, completely off balance, when suddenly his arm muscles gave out, and he fell into the water. Fortunately, he was wearing his life preserver.

"As soon as I hit the icy water I lost consciousness. The wind and waves carried me far away, but I was oblivious. . . . The alarm sounded, and someone sent a rowboat that, in spite of the distance and the waves, was able to recover me. I was pulled out of the water, given a bit of brandy, and taken back on board. I might have disappeared, carried away by the wind beyond the horizon and there, alone and unconscious, passed through this veil that separates earth and heaven. That sweet experience of the approach of death helped me, perhaps, to tame it."[5]

At the time, the incident seemed unimportant, and authorities neither investigated it nor asked Jean about it. "It was only long afterward," he says, "that I realized that I had been on the brink of dying." Reflecting on whether the event could explain his departure from the navy, he says, "That never occurred to me. I really don't know. I can't say yes; I can't say no. What is true is that during that whole time my spiritual life was being cultivated."[6] This spiritual life would, little by little, turn a naturally religious boy into a young man in search of absolutes.

A Spiritual Progression

IT WAS 1948, and Sub-Lieutenant Vanier had just finished his training cycle on torpedoes and cannons, first in his class. Soon, to the pride and joy of his parents, he was promoted to lieutenant and assigned to the *Magnificent*, the only Canadian aircraft carrier. He was succeeding brilliantly. He loved his profession. He was appreciated by his superiors and his comrades. And yet he felt an increasing pull toward something else. In two years he would leave the navy. What happened? "A spiritual progression," he would later say.

This spiritual progression came from various influences: his deeply religious family, who put their faith into action; decisive choices by loved ones that made a deep impression on him; and several significant encounters. His spiritual evolution would weave together three threads – an increasing desire for prayer, a growing attraction to the poor, and a hunger for community – that would intertwine throughout his life.

But why did Jean leave the navy? Had he had enough of these death machines he had learned to handle, or enough preparation for combat that never came? Did a growing love for peace cause him to become a pacifist? "No," he says, "I was never against the military. That was not possible in my family. Quite the opposite, I had an immense respect for those who had fought. . . . There are just wars. Nazism and barbarity had to be opposed, and the weak had to be defended. That's what we thought in my home, and that's what I thought. But one thing was certain: I couldn't see myself spending my whole life in the armed forces. I couldn't imagine being cloistered all my life on a warship. When I went to Paris on vacation with my parents I was in another milieu, an environment that was quite open and that offered me a more global view of the world."

After the war, during the time of reconstruction, there was a passionate intellectual and political ferment in France. At the embassy, Georges and Pauline Vanier received former members of the resistance, diplomats, politicians, intellectuals, and clergy, all of which enthralled the young Vanier.

"It was at the home of my parents that I met Jacques Maritain and got to know the nuncio Angelo Roncalli, the future Pope John XXIII, who became a friend of the family. After I left the navy and settled in France, Angelo Roncalli, who had been promoted to Patriarch of Venice, invited me to spend several days at his home. At Vézelay, where we vacationed, I also got to know Rosalie Vetch, the inspiration for Paul Claudel's character Ysé in his play *Partage de midi*. It was all so diverse, interesting, varied . . . and opened my spirit to things other than the navy. And then, inside me there was this yearning..."[7]

A yearning for what? It is difficult for him to say. His voice stops. For silence, no doubt, also for prayer, for the presence of God, certainly. He who in 2013 defined L'Arche as "a place of silence, of the Presence" had for a long time been inhabited by that yearning without really being conscious of it. In Montreal, in 1940, when his parents attended daily Mass, he willingly went along with them, and he accompanied them in 1946 at Vézelay when they attended their daily half-hour prayer. What happened inside him during these long moments of prayer from the ages of twelve to eighteen, when he attended Mass, or contemplated the Blessed Sacrament on the altar? For Catholics, the host, a white consecrated wafer in the monstrance, is the body of Christ – the real, substantial presence of Jesus himself. In the half-light of the church, lit only by a few altar candles, Jean waited in silence. There was nothing there that would usually attract the interest of an adolescent. But there he was.

When Jean thinks back to these years, he does not recall great mystical leaps, but only his faithfulness to the Eucharist and the increasing importance that it had in his life. In Greenwich, where he received naval training, he went to Mass every day. Before that he had taken long bike rides or hikes to find a church where he could receive communion. "For quite a while," he says, "my behavior was unusual for a young officer. It wasn't normal to go looking for a church upon entering a port, while everyone else went dancing. In any case, I wasn't comfortable with all that – the outings and distractions. None of that interested me. I think I had a religious streak – and some integrity as well. I wasn't divided. I was completely taken up with my faith and had the feeling that religion was more important than anything else – at least more than anything in the secular world."

In keeping with this outlook, Jean the naval officer got involved in the army – in this case, the Salvation Army! Over Christmas in 1949, when the *Magnificent* was based in Halifax, Jean spent all his free time distributing gifts to the disadvantaged of the city. He even borrowed a navy vehicle to help with transport – which resulted in a gentle but firm reprimand.

THE MOST STRIKING THING about the young Jean was his freedom. This personal freedom seemed to be rooted in his self-confidence and the trust that his father had shown him. In seeking to find a church at every port of call, the young man was acting like a lover in search of his beloved. The daily Mass, far from being an obligation he had to fulfill or a rite to be followed, was for him a meeting place. Beyond all the religious habits cultivated in his upbringing, Jean sought a personal experience of the presence of God.

René Girard says of mystical experience that the "first characteristic is its passive, involuntary nature. It is not preceded by any warning and does not require any effort. A second characteristic is joy. A third is a feeling of eternity that cannot be separated from its infinite power of renewal, its extraordinary fertility. The last characteristic combines all the others, and that is an intuition of a divine presence."[8] Early one morning during 1948, near a lake, Jean Vanier had such an experience. He was flooded with feelings of joy and peace, of being fulfilled. He knew then that he would leave the navy one day, not to do good deeds or for self-fulfillment, but to follow someone who called him: Jesus. Later, without speaking directly about himself, he often mentioned in his books and speeches this privileged moment of encounter, when one hears God say, as he said to the prophet Isaiah: "Since you were precious in my sight, you have been honored, and I have loved you."[9]

And so, in *Befriending the Stranger*, Jean Vanier writes:

> During one of our community weekends in northern France, an assistant asked Frank, a man with disabilities, if he prayed.
> He answered, "Yes."

"What do you do when you pray, Frank?"

"I listen."

"What does God say to you?"

"God says to me, 'You are my beloved son,'" he replied.

... The discovery that God loves us today ... and that today he says to us, "Follow me," is a great mystery.[10]

Not content to attend daily Mass – there was a chaplain on the *Magnificent* – and to say his prayers morning and evening, the young officer started regularly reading, as monks do, the Divine Office: matins, lauds, prime, terce, sext, none, vespers, and compline. The contemplative life of a monk is punctuated by the Office from early in the morning to bedtime, and even in the middle of the night. While on the aircraft carrier, with the aid of the Book of Hours, Jean Vanier recited the endless litany of the Psalms. One night while he was on watch, he surprised himself by standing an additional watch to assure the smooth running of the ship. Although he was conscientious and responsible, the officer recited the night office instead of concentrating on his task and following the navigation instruments. The young man in uniform watched the screens of the instruments that were tracing the ship's route, yet this was no longer the route he was following.

Decisive Influences

SILENCE, PRAYER, AND THE PRESENCE – the presence of God and of his guardian angels – seem to have traced an obvious path to a monastery. Like his older brother. Like Elizabeth de Miribel.

His brilliant older brother Georges, known as Byngsie to his friends, enlisted in 1944 at the end of his secondary studies and rejoined his parents in France at the beginning of 1946. They imagined he would pursue a career as a politician, diplomat, or philosopher. But on the feast of Saint Bernard, August 20, 1946, he announced his intention to enter the Trappist monastery of Notre-Dame-du-Lac in Oka, south of Montreal. And, in October, shortly before his twenty-first birthday, he entered and took the name of Brother Benedict.

Jean Vanier was not very close to his brother, but he was affected by Georges's decision, by the pride and admiration that his parents showed, by their fleeting anxiety in the face of this radical choice, and probably by a veiled fear of separation. The Trappists are a branch of the Cistercians, an order that was founded by Saint Bernard in the twelfth century. They follow a very strict, ascetic rule. The cloistered monks did not go out, so there would no longer be any family celebrations or vacations together. Brother Benedict, in place of the career that was expected, chose the desert of the monastery, silence, and a hidden life.

Elizabeth de Miribel, a family friend whom the Vaniers had met in Canada in 1942, was General de Gaulle's secretary in London. It was she who typed his famous speech of June 18, 1940. She entered a Carmelite convent in 1949. Jean Vanier and Elizabeth had already been corresponding, and Jean remembers going to visit her in her convent when he was on leave. The Carmelites, the order of Teresa of Avila and Thérèse of Lisieux, were also a cloistered, contemplative order. After all the adventures with the Free French, working as a war correspondent in Italy and France, and covering the liberation of Paris, Elizabeth chose a life of silence and prayer.

Jean could have followed the example of Byngsie and Elizabeth, but in addition to his longing for silence he also had a persistent attraction to the poor and downtrodden. This made a 1948 sojourn to Lourdes with his father all the more important. Lourdes, France, is a popular pilgrimage destination, where the sick and infirm can bathe in healing springs said to flow from a rock grotto where the Virgin Mary appeared to a peasant girl, Bernadette Soubirous, in 1858. Jean accompanied his father to the springs, helped him undress, and removed his prosthesis. "It was very moving for me to help him," he says. He was also moved by the humility of that man who was so important socially, and his simple acceptance of his infirmity. He was stripped naked, both physically and spiritually, when his son had to help him dip in that icy spring water. Again, Jean experienced the Presence, along with the experience of the fragility and dependence that comes with a sickness or handicap.

The grotto at Lourdes can incite fear. Countless abandoned crutches and prostheses hang suspended on a wall blackened by candle smoke. The crowd of sick and infirm, in wheelchairs and on stretchers, can fill one with horror. And yet the young officer left not horrified but moved. Later, Lourdes would become an important pilgrimage destination for the L'Arche community. The organization Faith and Light would be founded there, and it was there that the anniversaries of the movement would be celebrated.

ATTRACTED TO THE POOR and excluded, the young Jean was greatly influenced by several colorful figures who overturned conventions and battled prejudice. One of these was Dorothy Day, whom Jean Vanier calls "an extraordinary woman." Born in Brooklyn in 1897, she led the life of a bohemian activist in New York City. She was an anarchist and antimilitarist, committed to pacifist movements and women's suffrage. After she converted to Catholicism in 1927, she founded a newspaper, the *Catholic Worker*, and established hospitality houses to serve the destitute in poorer neighborhoods of New York City. In 1941, there were more than thirty Catholic Worker communities, and today there are over a hundred throughout the world. Dorothy Day was driven by her conscience and convictions. She was not satisfied with the world as it was, and labored for change in spite of the obstacles. Nor did she hesitate to criticize men of the church whom she found to be lukewarm. For instance, she vehemently opposed the cardinal of New York. In 1972, she received the Pacem in Terris Peace and Freedom Award, which Jean Vanier also received in 2013.

Jean readily associates Dorothy Day with a thirty-six-year-old Austrian farmer who demonstrated the same capacity to resist against all odds. Franz Jägerstätter was a Catholic and a father of three daughters. When he refused to enlist in the army and fight for Nazi Germany, despite pleas of "sensible" friends and relatives and his bishop, he was beheaded.

Jean also admired Catherine de Hueck Doherty, a Russian Orthodox baroness who was driven from her home during the Bolshevik Revolution. She became a nurse during World War I, moved to England, converted to Catholicism, and embarked for Canada in 1921, along with her husband and son. She took on jobs such as house cleaning and washing laundry in order to earn a living, until her fortunes changed and she grew rich and successful through public speaking. But she followed Christ's injunction, "Go, sell all you have, give the proceeds to the poor and follow me." She sold everything and went to live among the poor, welcoming them into her first Friendship House in Toronto in 1930. She was outspoken, and what she said about the gospel did not please the Catholic establishment very much. "She had a strong voice, strong convictions, and strong things to say," writes Thomas Merton, "and she was saying them in the simplest, most unvarnished, bluntest possible kind of talk, and with such uncompromising directness that it stunned."[11] Her house was shut down in 1936 by an ecclesiastical cabal. After a short time in Europe, she settled in New York City to found a new Friendship House in Harlem where blacks and whites would live together in community.

Stopover in New York

JEAN VANIER DISCOVERED the story of Catherine de Hueck Doherty in Thomas Merton's autobiography, *The Seven Storey Mountain*, a passionate book in which the Trappist monk tells the story of his agitated youth, his conversion to Catholicism, and his journey toward a monastic vocation. Merton's admiration for Doherty – more, his certainty that her life was directed by God – leapt from the pages that the young officer read while aboard the *Magnificent*. Doherty was motivated by the same vision as Dorothy Day, one that would also prevail in L'Arche: "There was to be nothing special about it," Merton writes of Friendship House, "nothing that savored of a religious order, no special rule, no distinctive habit. She, and those who joined her, would simply be poor . . . but they would embrace their poverty, and the life of the proletariat in all its misery and insecurity and dead, drab monotony. They would live and work in the slums, lose themselves, in the huge anonymous mass of the forgotten and the derelict, for the only purpose of living the complete, integral Christian life in that environment – loving those around them, sacrificing themselves for those around them, and spreading the gospel and the truth of Christ most of all by being saints, by living in union with him, by being full of his Holy Ghost, his charity."[12]

After a stop in Cuba, the *Magnificent* headed for New York in April of 1950. No sooner had he disembarked than the young uniformed officer, following in the footsteps of Thomas Merton, hurried toward Friendship House in Harlem. The household had grown considerably – to the great displeasure of the landlord – since the time Doherty, in search of a room, had settled with her typewriter and a little suitcase. It now filled several floors, and next to the lodgings a library, game room, and locker room had been built. "I was immediately captivated," remembers Jean Vanier. "Captivated," he repeats, "by that community, that happy community! Their joy, their happiness . . . I didn't want to leave, and I spent the entire time during the port of call, the whole week, with them. I even bought an enormous leg of lamb for Easter dinner and invited them to the aircraft carrier. Just imagine . . . those twenty poor people, whites and blacks, very simple, happy people strolling in the passageways of the *Magnificent* and relaxing in the officers' quarters!"[13]

CAPTIVATED – TO USE HIS WORD – by Friendship House, and confirmed in his desire for a life change, Jean Vanier resigned from his career in the Canadian Navy. Georges Vanier, showing again the great confidence he had in his son's intuition, wrote to the chief of staff who was worried about the decision: "Jock's aspirations transcend human horizons. Knowing him as I do, I'm sure that he is obeying a call from God. Since you have had the kindness to ask me my impressions, I can tell you simply that this is a matter between him and God in which we mustn't meddle."[14] On his return from Halifax, where the *Magnificent* was moored, Jean went to see his spiritual director, Father Daly. He wanted to become a priest and join Friendship House, so Father Daly recommended he go on a spiritual retreat at the Jesuit monastery in Montreal. He also suggested that the young man not commit himself right away, but take a year for study and prayer in order to see things more clearly. It was now 1950, and he had spent eight years in the navy. Where would he go? His mother suggested he visit Eau Vive (Living Water), a community of students in Soisy-sur-Seine, near Paris.

3

Disciple

JEAN VANIER DECIDED to move into Eau Vive for a year of meditation and prayer. Even though he had begun studying theology in preparation for the priesthood, he thought of himself not, first of all, as a student or seminarian, but as a man in search of God. He wanted the same thing that Jesus' first two followers in the Gospels wanted, which Jean Vanier describes in his book *Drawn into the Mystery of Jesus through the Gospel of John*:

> They do not want any ideas or theories.
> They do not want to be students.
> They want to enter into a relationship with Jesus,
> to *be with* him, stay with him.
> ... They want to become his disciples or followers.[1]

Compared with his other life choices – joining the navy at thirteen and leaving it at twenty-two – choosing Eau Vive seemed a simple choice. And yet, when looking at it more closely, that was far from the case.

Why Eau Vive? Why France? Jean Vanier did not speak French very well. His parents were perfectly bilingual. They had learned the two languages from earliest childhood. Unlike them, Jean spoke English and only learned French in school. His friends and acquaintances were mostly Canadian or English. His sister lived in

England, his older brother in Canada. Of course, his parents and grandmother now lived in France with his younger brother, so he would be closer to them. But it is difficult to imagine that being a determining factor for a man who had been able to leave home without a tear at the age of thirteen.

He didn't realize that upon arriving in Soisy-sur-Seine in September 1950 he would begin fourteen years of joy and discovery, but also of tribulation, loneliness, and exile. Jean, who up to now had only known success, would now experience hardship. After two peaceful years, for twelve difficult years he would be pruned – to take up the vocabulary of the vine and vine dresser in the Gospels – wounded, and stripped in preparation for becoming the founder of L'Arche.

JEAN'S STORY CAN BE SEEN as a classic example of election and promise, like those in the Old Testament. Of course, it is hard to compare a contemporary life to those fabulous stories of early prophets and patriarchs. But in truth, doesn't God work in lives today just as he did in the Bible, opening doors and revealing new paths? The Bible, for believers, is not just a story of olden times; it is also a story in which we interpret our own history in order to understand it and discern its course.

When he arrived at Eau Vive, the sailor known as "Jock" became Jean. But there was no divine intervention here, as when Abram became Abraham or Jacob became Israel. "Jock" sounds like "Jacques," the French name for James. So Jean requested a return to his baptismal name.

Jean did not claim that God changed his name as Abraham's had been. Yet his story reflects the deeper meaning of God's call to Abraham: "Go from your country, your people, and your father's household to the land I will show you. I will make you into a great nation, and I will bless you; I will make your name great, and you will be a blessing."[2] By simply following his intuition, this is the path that the future founder of L'Arche followed. He left his country, his relatives, and his father's house. He went to a foreign country and to an unknown people to which he would be introduced – people with intellectual disabilities. They are a great people, these disabled people of L'Arche who are so numerous today and whose hidden greatness Jean Vanier would reveal. For them – and many others – he was indeed a blessing.

Life at Eau Vive

EAU VIVE WAS SITUATED in a beautiful park with centuries-old trees. In addition to three large houses, there were student barracks. Among those who supported the establishment and taught courses there were Jacques Maritain; Charles Journet, the future cardinal; Monsieur de Moléon, professor at the Catholic Institute of Paris; and Olivier Lacombe, specialist in India and the Vedanta.

Jean met the founder of Eau Vive, Father Thomas Philippe. He was a Dominican and a scholar of Aquinas who had been a professor at the Pontifical University of Saint Thomas Aquinas before settling in the village of Étiolles and founding Eau Vive in 1947. Father Thomas wanted to create a "house of wisdom" and a "school of the heart." As a house of wisdom, Eau Vive gathered lay students who wanted to study philosophy and theology. They took courses at Saulchoir, the Dominican school of theology, which was within walking distance. As a school of the heart, Eau Vive was a community where prayer and brotherly life with the poor were essential to spirituality. It was not just a question of studying charity, but of putting it into daily practice. In the wake of the war, Eau Vive was an international school of peace where all would be welcome, no matter their age, origin, or religion. The school welcomed lay people who wanted to study theology, whether they were Muslim, Catholic, or Protestant. It was a project that seemed wildly ahead of its time.

When Jean arrived at Eau Vive, there were eighty students from some twenty countries. About twenty of the students came from the Arab countries of Syria, Lebanon, Egypt, and Morocco. His fellow students were mostly older than he was. Two or three were priests, and most were already doctoral candidates between the ages of twenty-five and thirty. They welcomed the young man and gave him a room in one of the barracks. He arranged his few belongings and went to see Father Thomas, who received him in his tiny office and suggested he study Latin.

And so began a nearly classic student life. Jean Vanier enjoyed living in the Eau Vive community: he took courses in philosophy and theology at Saulchoir, studied Latin, read spiritual classics, worked in the garden, and attended daily Mass. He particularly valued a newfound love for silence. "Teresa of Avila spoke about the prayer of quiet," Jean says. "A very beautiful word, quiet. It retains something of the physical. The whole body is in a state of silence, repose. Simply sitting down is sufficient and . . . being contented, without ideas, without thoughts, just simply being contented! I experienced that in a strong way."[3]

It is indeed in this way that Saint Teresa of Avila writes about the prayer of quiet. She writes that it "gives the soul the profound sensation of tasting happiness and peace." She added that this second grade of prayer – the first being vocal prayer, where the soul is conscious of itself and its efforts to draw closer to God – is "a little spark of the true love of himself, which our Lord begins to kindle in the soul." She continues, "This little spark is a sign or pledge which God gives to a soul, in token of his having chosen it for great things, if it will prepare to receive them. It is a great gift, much too great for me to be able to speak of it."[4]

A Spirituality of Love

IN ADDITION TO A SPIRITUALITY of quiet, Jean learned a spirituality of love. He grew in prayer that went beyond the recitation of texts and faithful adherence to doctrine. Jean remembers, "My intelligence, my understanding of God did not, then, develop starting from a doctrine, but from the mystical certainty of the presence of God."[5] Like the faith of Francis de Sales, Thérèse of Lisieux, and Teresa of Avila, whose works he read with passion, Jean learned a religion of love, gentleness, and trust.

That spirituality of love resonated with the faith of Jean Vanier's mother and grandmother. Jean's father had been raised with a purist understanding of religion that emphasized mistakes more than mercy. While Georges Vanier shared his wife's deep faith, for a long time his religious practice was "inspired more by fear than by love," writes Jean. "He only took communion two or three times each year, immediately after going to confession, for fear of not being pure enough to partake of his Lord."[6] Pauline led him little by little to view his faith in a different light – to perceive communion not as a reward for moral purity but as a necessary support in weakness, and prayer not as an obligation but as the vital dialogue of love. She introduced him to the writings of the mystics, such as John of the Cross and Teresa of Avila. Gradually this milieu, with which she had been familiar since childhood, opened Georges to a path that, henceforth, they would travel together.

When Jean was ten years old, his father went from attending Mass only on Sunday to daily celebration, with a half hour of prayer that would come to be important for the couple and their children. Georges Vanier discovered that gentleness and trust could accompany rigor and rectitude, that God's will is tender, and that it is better to trust God than to be afraid of one's mistakes. He began to understand the spirituality of Francis de Sales, who writes that it is sufficient to "be like little children: as long as they feel their mother holding onto their cuff, they go forth boldly and run around. They are not surprised by the little trifles they experience because of the weakness in their legs."[7]

The spirituality to which Jean Vanier subscribes is indeed in a direct line of descent from Francis de Sales and Thérèse of Lisieux.

Carmel, the cloistered monastery of Thérèse, and the silent and invisible prayer of its cloistered contemplative nuns play an essential role in the history of L'Arche and the life of Jean Vanier. He was touched when he discovered that Saint Thérèse, speaking of her monastery, called it "my dear ark." He saw in that a spiritual link between his movement and Carmel. For many years, he regularly visited Carmel both in Abbeville and in Cognac. As he became a world traveler, in the limelight as the voice of L'Arche, a mysterious union grew between him and the women of Carmel who silently, day after day, assisted him through prayer.

Director of Eau Vive

THE YOUNG MAN CONTINUED to discern what path he should follow. He was more and more attracted to prayer and, in February of that same year of 1951, he spent about ten days at La Valsainte Charterhouse in Switzerland, a Carthusian monastery that was well known to Charles Journet and Jacques Maritain. The place was magnificent. Someone came to fetch him in a horse cart that advanced slowly in the snow. The daily life of the Carthusians – prayer, study, and manual work in solitude and absolute silence – charmed him. He was happy at La Valsainte, but in leaving he knew he would never return. It was not his place. "I was still happier at Eau Vive."[8] Happiness! That is a word that is frequently on Jean Vanier's lips and one that explains his choices. Happiness – being happy together – would become the motto of L'Arche.

Jean made his decision. He would stay at Eau Vive. He would continue to pursue his theological studies, and when the time came, he would return to the Quebec diocese, where he would follow the steps of ordination, becoming a deacon, then a priest, before moving on to full ministry.

But in April 1952 there was a catastrophe at Eau Vive. Father Thomas was brusquely summoned to Rome. This was a thunderclap for Jean, who suspected nothing. He wasn't told what the authorities in Eau Vive and Saulchoir were dealing with. Father Thomas was not the type to confide. Jean lived in his barracks, studied, spent long hours in silent prayer, and worked in the garden. Father Thomas was dealt with severely. He was forbidden to return to Eau Vive, to teach, and to celebrate Mass or any other sacrament. Whether or not his condemnation had been fair, Father Thomas accepted it and disappeared. As he was leaving, he appointed Jean Vanier as director of Eau Vive. Everyone had expected Father Thomas to entrust Eau Vive to the mature, eminent psychiatrist Dr. John Thompson. Yet here he had chosen Jean, twenty-four years old, with no experience in the management of a school and spiritual center or in taking charge of a community. This mark of trust, following that of his father when he wanted to join the navy, was a renewed confirmation of his capabilities.

The young idealist, raised in a family where honor and uprightness were self-evident, and trained by the military, where esprit de corps trumped personal interests, was soon to be brutally plunged into a sadly banal world of intrigue, pettiness, and settling of scores. The Dominicans wanted to regain control of Eau Vive and appoint their own director. The board of directors of Eau Vive refused their nomination and approved the nomination of Jean Vanier. Striking back, the Dominicans immediately forbade the students at Eau Vive to take classes at Saulchoir. The tree was cut off at the roots. One after another, the students deserted Eau Vive. Soon there were no more than fifteen left. They enrolled in the Catholic Institute of Paris. Among them was Jean. He continued with his courses and held faithfully to the post that had been entrusted to him. Stubbornness and pigheadedness, his accusers would say. Where did he find the strength to oppose the authorities and to resist pressure?

He had, of course, the example of his father, who held out for three years in the trenches and returned to combat after he was wounded. This son of a general, who was himself an officer, also had somewhat of a fascination with rebels. His personal pantheon was populated with people who had crossed swords with those in authority and had been punished: resisters such as Catherine de Hueck Doherty, expelled from her first Friendship House; Dorothy Day, imprisoned for civil disobedience; and Franz Jägerstätter and Dietrich Bonhoeffer,[9] executed by the Nazis. These were his role models in the fifties.

In 1953, Jean met a man in Montreal who also impressed him profoundly: Tony Walsh. He was a prophet, Jean Vanier says. This Irishman born in Paris was raised in England and Scotland. He emigrated to Canada after the First World War, becoming a teacher on an Okanagan reservation. Fascinated by Native American culture, he encouraged the children to reclaim their heritage, speak their language, and rediscover their dances, songs, and designs – all this at a time when the government was attempting to turn the Indians into good Canadians. Turned out of the reservation by security forces, Tony Walsh arrived in Montreal in 1949. He threw himself into establishing a house of hospitality for street people, the Benedict Labre House, which opened in 1952. Pauline Vanier sometimes went there to serve meals, and Jean helped there during his vacations.

Beyond these models and examples, the young man's steadfastness was rooted in his faith. It was by remaining in Jesus Christ that Jean Vanier renewed his strength. He turned to God, who gives strength to resist pressure and grace to accept the loss of everything in order to hold to what one believes.

In 1955, Eau Vive, the bishop of Versailles, and the Dominican order reached an agreement. The students would be able to return to Saulchoir to study. Jean would remain as director of Eau Vive, and he was given a chaplain as an assistant. The young director, however, continued to defend the heritage and spirituality of Father Thomas, while the chaplain wanted to make his own mark, so a conflict was inevitable. In June 1956, Jean Vanier was kicked out. He was given three weeks to leave. No one cared where he would live or how he would support himself. His parents had already returned to Canada. All he had left in France were his grandmother and his brother Bernard, who had launched a career as a painter. His training for the priesthood was also brought into question.

For the first time in his life, Jean Vanier did not know where to go or what to do. He no longer knew what path to take – no certainty, no course outlined, no plans. "On this journey, when you get lost, that is when you are finally on the way," writes John of the Cross. That was a true but harsh lesson for Jean. Night, silence, and solitude. Eight years of wandering followed. For all that, the young man was not particularly anxious. He was calm and seemed to happily appreciate this time of solitude, even though he couldn't stand still. He had a pragmatic outlook that adapted easily to new circumstances. He knew only one thing for sure: he wanted to follow Jesus.

And so, little by little, through twists and turns, the various elements that would lead to the creation of L'Arche came together like the pieces of a puzzle.

On This Path

IN SEPTEMBER 1956, Jean Vanier settled in the Bellefontaine Cistercian abbey in the French department of Vendée. Bellefon-taine was the mother community of the Oka abbey in Canada, where his elder brother Benedict lived. Jean lived at the guest house, a large, beautiful stone building. While there, he took part in the services and worked in the garden, but he did not enter completely into the life of the monks: most of his time was dedicated to personal prayer and study. Life in the guest house was simple, but for a long time Jean Vanier had felt called to a life of poverty. He owned nothing to speak of, having given away all he had when he left the navy. Even when he arrived at Eau Vive, all he had brought were a few books. He was not afraid of manual labor. He worried little about what he ate and was concerned neither about the beauty of his surroundings nor his personal comfort.

However, life at the monastery still seemed too comfortable for him. Within a year, he chose greater poverty and solitude as he settled in a little house with no facilities in the Normandy countryside at Crulai, in the department of Orne. He found the house one day as he was passing through the town of L'Aigle on his way back to Bellefontaine. Stopping, he asked if there might be a secluded, inexpensive house for rent in the area.

The house was downright dilapidated. It had hardly any heating, and water needed to be drawn from a well. Mice pranced around between the joists, running across the peeling wallpaper and falling on his bed. It was raining mice – and water, too, in the corners of the room! But the house, located about ten kilometers from the village, was completely isolated.

Jean went to Mass every morning in the surrounding churches, but he did not try to meet the priests or anyone else; he slipped away discreetly at the end of the services. He lived the simple life of a hermit, happy in his solitude. Up early each morning for prayer, he loved to watch the sun rise. He took walks during the day, cultivated his little garden plot, and worked on his thesis on Aristotle, which he had begun at the Catholic Institute of Paris. Each evening, he went to bed early because the light was bad and it was cold, but also because the great barrenness of the countryside frightened him a bit. He became simpler. Little by little his desire for excellence, success, and recognition faded. He renounced his ambition to become a priest. He accepted not knowing where this path was leading him.

He seemed to be following, without knowing it, the same path as the French hermit and spiritual master Charles de Foucauld, who went from the military to the Trappists at Notre-Dame-des-Neiges, then to a hermitage, passing through a little gardener's house in Nazareth that belonged to the order of St. Clare. After Jean's time at the Trappist monastery of Bellefontaine and his Norman house, he, too, went to live in a little garden cottage, which belonged to American nuns in Fatima, Portugal. He lived a semi-hermetic life there for two years.

In Fatima, Jean rose very early. He would be sitting in front of the Blessed Sacrament in the basilica by four in the morning, and would stay for Mass. Then, after running a few errands, he would return home to eat, work, and pray. He loved his solitude. Even so, he once agreed to be the guide for some Nigerian pilgrims, and gave language lessons every Monday to an elderly priest named Father Reis. Father Reis spent his days in his confessional and wanted very much to hear the confession of English pilgrims. He was charming and diligent, but the language of Shakespeare didn't stick with him very well. There was also a cobbler neighbor who, while resoling shoes, was waiting for the end of the world. He would rush euphorically to Jean Vanier's home as soon as he heard about any catastrophe to announce to him that the last days were near.

Jean's similarity to Charles de Foucauld extended beyond living in a gardener's house. The spirituality of the "universal brother," as Foucauld was known, also nurtured that which was deepening in Jean – another thread to interweave with those of Thérèse of Lisieux, Teresa of Avila, and Francis de Sales. In 1953, while vacationing in Montreal with his parents, Jean had met the Little Sisters of Jesus, the order founded in 1939 by Sister Magdeleine. Every Thursday, he went with his parents to pray in the chapel of these disciples of Charles de Foucauld. There, in the silence, Jean Vanier again felt the presence of God, and the life of these unassuming nuns touched him as well. They lived among the poor and in the same manner as the poor, offering their friendship to all. That buried, silent, hidden presence was modeled on the hidden life of Jesus during his thirty years of silence in Nazareth. In

Montreal, Jean met Sister Monique, who then introduced him to the founder, Sister Magdeleine. The friendship and life these sisters shared with the poor stemmed from the same vision that had motivated Tony Walsh, Dorothy Day, and Catherine de Hueck Doherty. This was also, of course, the vision of Charles de Foucauld, for whom the important thing was "not to convert, but to be with"[10] and, in imitation of Jesus, to seek the lowliest place.

One day, Jean Vanier would find that lowliest place, where Jesus dwells, with people with intellectual disabilities. At this point, he was not yet aware of that; he was still quite far from the world of those with disabilities. For the moment, in his prayerful solitude, he worked on his dissertation – "Happiness as the Principle and End of Aristotelian Ethics." He made short trips to Paris to meet with his dissertation committee. He was happy.

Then suddenly Jean fell quite ill with a serious case of hepatitis. Doctors counseled him to rest in the mountains, so he packed up his books, left his little house in Fatima, and headed for Switzerland. Driving around at random through the town of Törbel, he inquired about a house to rent, and ended up in an alpine chalet where he stayed until the spring of 1961. Then he went back to Paris, finished his dissertation, and defended it in June 1962. He graduated cum laude from the Catholic Institute of Paris with the degree of Doctor of Theology.

Trosly-Breuil

IN 1959, JEAN VANIER'S FATHER had been appointed governor general of Canada. In the official photo, His Excellence Georges Philias Vanier, the highest dignitary in the country, looks handsome. He wears a uniform studded with the crosses of various orders for which he was grand chancellor, along with an impressive display of ribbons, the most prestigious of which were earned on the battlefield. He rests his hand on the pommel of his sword and stands, looking straight ahead. Pauline Vanier has the mien and look of a queen in her dress made of burgundy velvet. She is also decorated with medals and a river of diamonds and long earrings. They had settled in Ottawa, where they met up with Jean whenever he came to see them. Quite another world!

Meanwhile, Father Thomas had regained the right to celebrate the sacraments, but he remained in exile. Neither the Dominicans nor the church seemed to want to entrust him with any mission. The psychiatrist Dr. Préaut, with whom he had collaborated at the Longueil-Annel school for young delinquents, offered him a position as chaplain of Val Fleuri in Trosly-Breuil, in the department of Oise. The former professor accepted this humblest of positions and became chaplain to thirty or so intellectually disabled men whose faith lives were a mystery. As for the team of caregivers, they were mostly quite anticlerical, and only grudgingly accepted the presence of a priest.

Val Fleuri, a little chateau located on a street named Rue d'Orléans, had been purchased by a Mr. Prat for his disabled son. With the aid of Dr. Préaut, he had turned it into an institution that welcomed other men with intellectual disabilities. Trosly and Breuil, two villages bordering a state-owned forest, had become one municipality. The church was located in Breuil, but Trosly was older. The contrast was striking between the main road, which trucks traveled day and night, and the bucolic charm of the village. The little streets that ran perpendicular to the highway snaked between the white-stone Picardy houses and the small, enclosed gardens toward the immense, shaded forest, from which deer regularly appeared.

Father Thomas moved into two miserable rooms near Trosly's Place des Fêtes in December 1963. He was poor both by choice and by necessity. Jean helped him to renovate the place and to set up a chapel in the larger of the two rooms. Jean attended the Christmas service at Val Fleuri, then headed off to Canada, where he had accepted a post as visiting professor of ethics at the University of Saint Michael's College, federated with the University of Toronto. The idea of teaching interested him. Yet several months later, he declined a tenured post at the university. "So I felt that the time had arrived," he later wrote. "I had no plans, I didn't know what I would be doing, but I suspected that events were evolving, and that something was about to transpire."[11]

4

Founder

SOMETHING WAS ABOUT TO TRANSPIRE. Jean Vanier had no plan. Father Thomas thought there was "something to do," that Jean might be able to "start something."[1] He was moved by the men with intellectual disabilities at Val Fleuri that he had come to know, by their simplicity and openness to God. "They are," Father Thomas would say, true disciples of Jesus: humble and poor, open to the influence of the Spirit," Jean Vanier says today, "Father Thomas saw in them little souls who give what is most important to Jesus: the heart."[2]

Jean had come away from his first meeting with the men of Val Fleuri with mixed feelings. The young philosopher was afraid – the same fear that he still feels upon visiting a prison, leprosarium, or any of these closed worlds. Yet other emotions were mixed in with the fear: a strange impression that was difficult to grasp overwhelmed him. When he walked into Val Fleuri, it was as though he had crossed a border, not only that border with visible bars, but another border that was deeper and invisible. He felt as though he was in another, unsettling, world. In the normal world he knew what he should do and how to act. But here, he no longer knew what to do or think. Because the men were putting on a Christmas play, it was all the more bewildering.

In the illusion and role-playing no one was who he seemed to be. Everything seemed strange to him.

"There was an attraction and a repulsion," he remembers. "An attraction toward a mystery and a repulsion from the abnormal. But over and above that, what charmed me was their crying out for friendship. They all fluttered around me like bees around flowers. They touched me and asked, 'Will you come back to see us?' I was moved when they asked, 'Are you coming back to see us again?' I heard this mute cry, a massive crying out for a relationship. It was something incredibly sweet. There was a certain fierceness among them, but in their contact with me there was this cry, a cry inviting me to be their friend. That is what touched me deeply – that call. I left for Canada to teach my classes, but I knew I would return. I didn't know where or how, but I had the feeling that something would come and that it was enough for me to let myself be guided."[3]

Jean returned to France the next spring, 1964. He visited care homes and psychiatric hospitals, and met with despairing parents. He was horrified by what he found: a world of neglect and misery, of violence and exclusion. In one place he found a young man chained up in a hayloft; in another he saw high, gray walls with barred metal gates, where dozens of phantoms in pajamas stared into a void. The healthcare workers and authorities were probably doing what they could, but these men, relegated to overcrowded asylums, were languishing, without any activities, without any hope. Everywhere he went he found this same expectation and heard the same plea: "Do you love me? Why have I been abandoned? Why am I not like my brothers and sisters who are married and who live in a house? Why am I here?"[4]

The young professor did not attempt to answer the "why." All his philosophy was silent. He didn't try to launch into any general explanation or large-scale project. He drafted no charter or strategy. He offered no solution to resolve the problem that these thousands of deprived people were facing. He had no plan. But he was committed to doing something. That cry – "Do you love me? Does somebody love me?" – haunted him. "Yes," he answered, "as for me, I love you and I am inviting you to live with me." The decision had been made, even though it seemed ridiculously small and insignificant. He would move to Trosly and buy a house. He would invite some men who were disabled and without families to live with him.

He knew that there was no backing out of what he was doing. It was out of the question to send the people he was welcoming back to the asylum one day, so he was committing his whole life to the project. The sailor was casting anchor once and for all. He was thus turning his back on many things: the pleasures of teaching, traveling, his precious freedom. He would no longer be able to pack his little car with bags and books and set out alone on an adventure. Then there was his solitude that was so fruitful and full, that made him so happy. But still, L'Arche was born. What a curious founder; what a curious foundation!

The Only Program

THE MATTER WAS DECIDED, and the moving date chosen: August 4, 1964. Jacqueline d'Halluin, who had been Father Thomas's secretary at Eau Vive, wrote a prayer for the occasion, which would become the prayer of L'Arche. This prayer, which Jean Vanier wanted written before anything else got underway, captured the spirit of what would be his whole program:

> O Mary,
> we ask you to bless our house,
> keep it in your Immaculate Heart,
> make L'Arche a true home,
> a refuge for the poor, the little ones,
> so that here they may find the source of all life,
> a refuge for those who are deeply tried,
> so that they may find your infinite consolation.

O Mary,
give us hearts that are attentive, humble and gentle,
so that we may welcome with tenderness and compassion
all the poor you send to us.
Give us hearts full of compassion
so that we can love, serve, dissolve all discord,
and see in our suffering and broken brothers
the humble presence of the living Jesus.

Lord, bless us by the hand of your poor.
Lord, smile on us through the gaze of your poor.
Lord, receive us one day in the happy company of your poor.

The prayer was written, but several questions remained. First of all, the house: by June, Jean had not yet found it. Next, finances: in order to purchase the house, he might have to count on his parents and friends, but even then, what would they live on? Lastly, the residents who would be entrusted to him: how would that be arranged?

Indeed, these were important questions that would have derailed many. But Jean Vanier did not think like everyone. As in his choice of the navy, he had "the certainty that this was what he had to do." He was also organized and efficient. He knew what he wanted, and knew on which doors to knock. And he wasn't alone: he had parents who were important and well known, as well as a network of relations and friends. Certainly, he was poor; he possessed few things and did not worry about earning money. But, having read Francis de Sales, he knew that, in fact, he was rich. His poverty was a chosen poverty, like that of the monks – a poverty that was honored, Francis had said, unlike the poverty of those who were looked down upon because they had failed to succeed in the world.

Jean was not ashamed of his poverty. He knew how to speak to the mighty; he knew how to speak to those in power and how to deal with the cogs in administrative wheels. He also knew how to ask for help when he needed it. "He always knew how to hit up important people and find allies," said Alain Saint Macary, former international coordinator of L'Arche. Poor though he was, Jean placed an intangible wealth – gained through his education, the trust of his father, his relationships, and his amazing energy – at the service of the poorest of the poor.

Jean also needed a board of directors. Dr. Préaut and Mr. Prat, administrators of SIPSA (Society for the Instruction and Protection of Children Who Are Deaf-Mute or Intellectually Disabled), a registered nonprofit organization, offered the services of their organization to manage his future foundation. He accepted on the condition that he take over the presidency and have the power to appoint half of the members of the administrative board. It was clear that he had political sense. He wanted to have a free hand and, before even knowing exactly what he wanted to do, he insured he would have the means of carrying out whatever needed to be done. The current president, granddaughter of the founder of SIPSA, willingly agreed to cede her place to him, so friends of Jean Vanier were appointed to the board at the beginning of July.

Jean also met the regional director of social services and the person responsible for care facilities for people with disabilities. Although Jean had no expertise or title, people trusted him, and at that time the needs were so great that the administration was ready to support any initiative. They were looking for alternative solutions to family care, asylums, psychiatric hospitals, and religious communities.

Jean Vanier was also familiar with the world of psychiatry and psychoanalysis. He was anything but naïve, and clearly distinguished between what he called compassion-competence and compassion-compassion. He often forcefully declared that if someone has a toothache, the best thing to do is not to say "I love you," but to take the person to the dentist. The young founder surrounded himself with people whose professional skills might be useful. Dr. Préaut was a renowned psychiatrist. Dr. Thompson, whom he saw from time to time at Eau Vive, was a pioneer of "Friendship Therapy." He was among those practitioners who contested psychiatric practices such as lobotomies and shock therapies, which had been in vogue since the 1940s for lack of effective medications. From almost the very beginning, there was a psychiatrist at L'Arche, not only to treat the patients but also to conduct review meetings with the assistants.

The First Home

JEAN FOUND THE HOUSE in July 1964. It was a small, white-stone house with a little yard, located outside the village. It was near the forest and not far from Val Fleuri. One evening in August, just after moving in, they chose a name. Jacqueline d'Halluin made a list of names taken from the Bible, and Jean Vanier settled on L'Arche. The French word *"arche"* has multiple meanings: Noah's Ark, but also the arch of a bridge flung across two worlds. It is even a name for Mary, Jean noted, whom the Church Fathers had called "the Ark of the Covenant" because she had carried the Savior in her bosom.[5]

The first members of the L'Arche community came from the Saint-Jean-les-Deux-Jumeaux care home. Jean had visited the home before the summer, and saw that the situation was dire. The director, Mrs. Martin, was a generous woman who could not refuse any parent or institution that approached her. She welcomed all the disabled with open arms into the asylum, a former convent, and ended up with eighty people crammed into two dormitories that had been designed for forty. The beds touched one another, and there was no place to stand. The small staff could hardly keep up with daily care. Jean Vanier was overwhelmed by the violence and sadness of the place.

Mrs. Martin was desperate. The administration had just demanded that she somehow make changes and reduce the number of occupants. So when a tall Canadian offered to take in some of the people, he seemed to be a godsend. On August 5, Mrs. Martin brought Philippe Seux, Raphaël Simi, and a third young man named Danny, who was severely disturbed and deaf-mute, to Trosly. Philippe and Raphaël had been placed in the asylum after the death of their parents. Philippe was twenty-three and had to walk with crutches because he was paralyzed on one side. Unlike Raphaël, who had been deprived of speech by meningitis, Philippe talked – in a flood of words whose meaning did not always align with reality. He dreamed of becoming a radio announcer. Philippe recounts: "The first time I met Jean Vanier it was in a center where we were not allowed to leave. I saw him in the chapel, then he served up the soup. He impressed me right away. I had the impression that the table was tiny because he was so tall."

Jean welcomed Philippe, Raphaël, and Danny to the first L'Arche home. He and an old friend of his, Jean-Louis Coic, had moved in the evening before. They had done what they could to fix up the house. Dr. Préaut gave them several pieces of furniture, and Jean had obtained a big table and a buffet. The plates, glasses, and silverware were all mismatched. The house had neither a bathroom nor hot water, but it at least had a cold water tap and a woodstove. For a toilet, they set up a bucket in the yard. They greeted one another, shared a meal that Mrs. Martin had brought, and then the guests departed.

NIGHT FELL. "We were a bit lost," Jean Vanier admits. They didn't know where to turn on the electricity, so they lit candles. Philippe slept in the only bedroom on the ground floor, because his disability prevented him from climbing the rickety ladder to the upper floor, which was a sort of attic where the others slept. Jacqueline d'Halluin had improvised cubicles and created some semblance of privacy by separating the beds with colorful drapes. She had also purchased a statue of the Virgin Mary in an antique shop in Compiègne and placed it in the large room.

The night was ghastly. Danny, lost in his dream world and suffering, couldn't understand where he was. Everything frightened him. He was hallucinating, writhing, getting up, walking back and forth, and going out into the street and howling. He kept everyone awake. They had to take him back to the care home the next morning. Failure and the first pain.

But the others were delighted. "When I came to L'Arche," Philippe Seux said, "there wasn't any electricity, nothing. We had to use candles – it was fun! There were no sanitary facilities or showers. I was so happy I exploded like a bomb: I felt so free! What I experienced before, for me, was no life, sitting all day in a room. We didn't have anything to do, we never went out, we were bored stiff: no activities, nothing. I even cried. I wasn't at all comfortable. Little by little things worked out at L'Arche. We started as best we could. We cooked together, and everyone helped make the meals. . . . After that there were jobs to do; we installed sanitary facilities. We felt free to take walks in the village. It was as though we were a tree around which a huge mushroom was growing. That was us!"[6]

The First Months

GRADUALLY, L'ARCHE BECAME more organized. Louis Pretty, a Canadian architect, and Henri Wambergue, a cousin of Father Thomas, joined the little group at the end of August. In his first newsletter, dated August 22, 1964, Jean announced that L'Arche had legally become a branch of Val Fleuri. "That means that we are authorized to receive financial aid. And in several months, we will apply to have L'Arche approved as a distinct center," he wrote.[7]

In that first newsletter, Jean Vanier also spelled out a plan for L'Arche. He mentioned the direction that the community would take: a family-style environment in little houses for individuals with intellectual and physical disabilities. It would not be enough to simply care for them, he wrote; L'Arche would be a place where they would "really be able to grow and develop according to their particular characters and aptitudes." He planned to create "workshops, a cultural center, and a chapel, as well as appropriate medical help." He maintained that there were two essential and related principles: firstly, that "L'Arche is a Catholic home, but religious practice is entirely free," and secondly, the importance of poverty. "These poorest of the poor" would be cared for by volunteers. "Together," he concluded, before soliciting concrete help from correspondents, "we want to create homes that radiate peace and joy in the spirit of the Beatitudes."[8]

Jean never imagined the breadth – in both significance and direction – that his project would take on. It was as though he had set in motion an enterprise that was higher than he was, yet for which he was responsible. He recalls, "This project exceeded by far anything that I could have imagined."[9] Of course, his understanding of situations, his pragmatism, his faith in people and in God, and his energy were determining factors. "My role was to welcome the events and let them guide me. Later I discovered that my ignorance and poverty at the beginning of L'Arche helped me be more attentive to God, and allowed him to guide me from day to day. If I had had a clear plan, I might have been less ready to welcome God's plan."[10]

In the meantime, the residents of L'Arche lived off help provided by friends, as well as aid provided by inhabitants of the village who were touched by this adventure. Parisians and former Eau Vive colleagues sent packages and came to lend a hand from time to time. Ms. Gsell, Mrs. Lepère, and Mrs. Morinvillé gave vegetables and apples from their gardens. Mr. Roland offered to do masonry work for free. Mrs. Bertrand brought soup every Friday. Antoinette Maurice, a social worker from Compiègne, was intrigued by Jean. She quoted her colleague Christine Edé, who said he was either "a saint or a loony." Still, the two women alternated cooking duties every other Monday.

Antoinette remembered, with emotion, the first meal she ate at L'Arche on August 25, 1964. The house was welcoming. Jean and his companions did not hesitate to invite just about anyone who came along. "What touched me," she wrote, "was not so much the menu as the atmosphere that reigned in that house." The menu, it is true, was a bit disconcerting. Jean was the one who did the cooking. He claimed he hadn't peeled the carrots so they would retain all their vitamins. The herring would have been improved by being thoroughly cooked – and the dessert served on a separate plate. But who cared? The social worker was touched by something altogether different: "Everyone participated according to their abilities: Philippe ground the coffee, Raphaël swept, and everyone helped with the dishes, including the guests. That atmosphere of attentiveness and joy incited me to return often."[11] In fact, Antoinette returned so often that she ended up moving to Trosly in 1970 to become assistant director of the community, before taking responsibility for the L'Arche community in Compiègne.

That inexplicable atmosphere of peace emanated from Jean Vanier. Even today, when leading the conversation at a meal, he promotes togetherness and bonhomie. While respecting those who are eating in silence, he does not let people withdraw. He introduces people to one another. He makes sure that each person, even those who are speech-impaired, has a chance to speak. He asks one person for the salt, asks another about her day, offers some water, hands around plates, and listens. He is present. He is loving. Peace and cheerfulness surround the table. The meal is quite simply "a little daily celebration."[12]

Alain Saint Macary, remembering his first meals at L'Arche, says that Jean had a real gift for keeping a conversation going:

> Sometimes the atmosphere could get a bit strained. Those just coming out of psychiatric hospitals were flustered by this new life. The budding community offered less security, treatment was less effective, psychiatric intervention less advanced. Jean would

facilitate conversations and then suddenly in the middle of a meal, if he felt things weren't going well, he would launch into a game by grabbing a dictionary, searching through the section with quotes and proverbs, then asking for the end of a proverb after giving the first line. Sometimes he would name a town and ask everybody to guess its population. Everyone participated, even guests, official or not. What delighted him was that often it was the disabled people who called out a number that came closest to being correct! As for Raphaël, he loved practical jokes and tricks. Jean had bought him a fake mustard jar out of which popped a horned devil. You had to see them, both of them, dying with laughter when the devil burst up into the nose of this or that person.[13]

Jean wasn't pretending. No doubt, in the beginning, this was not his kind of humor. It's hard to imagine that there had been pop-up mustard jars, drinking glasses that dripped, or whistling camembert cheeses at General Vanier's table. If he laughed, it was surely because Raphaël was laughing, and that laughter was infinitely precious to him. But it was also because in the little L'Arche house with Philippe, Raphaël, and soon Jacques Dudouit and Jean-Pierre Crépieux, everything took on a new aspect. "Normal" social orders were erased, the conception of what was important or not was modified, and the mirage of success was exposed for what it was: a deception. A breath of freedom, like a perpetual holiday, blew through the little home.

Jean, the deeply serious young man, was rediscovering child-hood. He led the nascent community, taking on remodeling projects, searching for funds, and, when it was his turn, cleaning and cooking. He helped Philippe bathe, calmed Raphaël's anxieties, looked into the creation of workshops, and conducted a Bible study once a week for a small group that gathered in the home. But he also enjoyed games that amused his companions. It was as though a heavy weight had fallen from his shoulders. With them, he was free to have a water fight, to play dress-up, and to joke around. They played bocce in the little courtyard, they sang, they juggled, they performed charades. They laughed about anything and everything around the fire in the evening. They were happy together.

The First Assistants

THE RESIDENTS OF L'ARCHE had won Jean's heart, and they soon captivated others as well. By 1965, the first assistants had arrived: Barbara Swanekamp, a young French teacher from New York; Annie Morinvillé; and Pierre Brunière. Alain Saint Macary, a brilliant businessman with a promising career, visited L'Arche weekend after weekend. He left his post at a bank for several months, then for a year, and finally for good, to work with L'Arche. And it was because of Raphaël that Odile Ceyrac committed herself to L'Arche.

At the first meal to which Odile had been invited by Mira, her young Indian friend who was responsible for the household, things had gone rather poorly. Raphaël, dirty, badly shaved, and drooling a bit, was in a bad mood. Sitting next to Odile, he turned his back while making little whimpering noises. As she spoke about her studies in international law she was feeling very uncomfortable. Suddenly, at the end of the meal, he turned around. He looked at her "with such a tenderness, such love" that she was shaken. "There was something quite extraordinary in his eyes," she added. "Something clear and deep, as though it were coming from far away, from the depths of time."[14] Through this expression of such sudden intensity, she felt called to spend her life at L'Arche with Raphaël and people like him.

The little initial group that had gathered in 1964 grew very naturally – one is tempted to say, as Philippe suggested, that it sprang up like a mushroom. Father Thomas's improvised chapel was too small to accommodate all the friends of L'Arche. Jean Vanier's correspondence from this period reveals an ambivalent feeling. He appealed to his friends, expressing a desire to create a larger community and envisioning being able to welcome older people with other types of disabilities. At the same time, he rejoiced that the size of the household allowed him to transport everyone in a single car.

"When I welcomed Raphaël and Philippe," he wrote in 1995, "I had no particular plan or precise ideas. I knew nothing about people with intellectual disabilities, but I had been moved by their suffering in the asylums and institutions I had visited. I wanted, for the sake of Jesus and the gospel, to help them find a more human and Christian life. I did not even have an idea of what a L'Arche community should be. As the days went by, I began to understand Raphaël's and Philippe's needs and to discover what community really meant. I think it would be difficult to find a founder less capable than I was. I tried to live each day as it came. . . . I was naïve, but determined. I wanted to work for Jesus and for his kingdom. I tried to be attentive to the way in which Providence was guiding me precisely because I did not really know what I was being asked to do!"[15]

The First Community

AN EXTRAORDINARY SITUATION would precipitate events. At the end of 1964, the entire staff of Val Fleuri quit because of a problem with their salaries. Dr. Préaut, who was president of the board of directors, asked Jean to take over the management of the center at the end of three months' notice. Here he was again, a director without wanting it or having any experience. He said yes, however, and continued to cultivate his little garden at L'Arche without worrying too much.

Jean flew to Canada in February of 1965. Since he was no longer free to teach full time, he had agreed to give lectures. At Toronto, as at other universities to which he was invited, he spoke to packed auditoriums on the subjects of art, friendship, love, and the cry of the poor. Many of the early assistants at Trosly, as well as many of the initial founders of new L'Arche communities, were Canadian students who had been touched by his words.

Upon his return to France, however, he found that there had been no preparation for the transition at Val Fleuri. On March 22, 1965, the departing director coolly handed him a ring of keys, showed him where to find the account books, and left. The rest of the staff – accountant, gardener, nurse, educators, and workshop managers – had already left. "I felt very much alone," he remembers. He then immediately reported that the keys had been either lost or stolen! He convinced a couple of the former educators to return for several months, and mobilized the village folk to help in the workshops, manage the accounts, and do the laundry. It took several weeks before he found a nurse. In the meantime, he was the one who gave shots to Denis, who was diabetic. In order to become familiar with the procedure, he practiced a whole evening on an orange!

Jean dug into the files and spent time getting to know the thirty-two residents. He had seen them at Christmastime in 1963, and again each time he brought Philippe and Raphaël to Val Fleuri to shower. He had also seen them walking in a row, two by two, in the streets of Trosly on their daily stroll. Now he slept on site – or rather kept watch, since nights were unpredictable and days were taken up with the headaches of hospital expenses, salaries, standards, inspections, and balance sheets.

Jean wanted to introduce the Val Fleuri residents to increased freedoms, but this was a delicate endeavor. As the community's cook said, "Before, it was much stricter; the guys were not allowed to go out alone. They stayed in the courtyard all the time. But Mr. Vanier immediately lost the keys and let the guys go out. The guys were very pleased about that. Before it was a prison, but now they had freedom. The guys were upset, though, because of the change in management. There were difficult moments: a lot of window panes were broken, and there were terrible fights."[16]

Jean Vanier remembers that it sometimes took four people to restrain someone. He was glad that his great height was helpful at such times. Of course, he wasn't alone. People in his little household, as well as people from the village, came to help. But the strength of his endurance, here as at Eau Vive, was striking. "Thinking about it today, I don't know how I held up," he writes. "It was crazy! We had so few assistants, while the men at Val Fleuri were very troubled and explosive. Fortunately, I was naïve. I had the impression that Jesus was present in all the difficulty and the chaos, and that he would help us. It was only by God's grace that I was able to hold up, because humanly it was impossible."[17]

VAL FLEURI WAS a specialized institution, while the little L'Arche household welcomed the poor after the example of Catherine de Hueck Doherty's Friendship House or of Tony Walsh's Benoît-Labre House. The L'Arche prayer expresses it clearly, ". . . welcome with tenderness and compassion all the poor you send to us." The little house in Trosly was open to all.

Yet Jean soon realized it was impossible to indiscriminately welcome any and all who came along. Those who were there already had to be protected. On Christmas Eve in 1964, Jean came across a vagabond on the road to Compiègne. He invited him to spend several days with them and to come back whenever he wanted. Gabriel was amusing and capricious, but when he came back in February for a longer visit they found him to be agitated, unstable, and jealous. Moreover, he was violent toward Philippe and Raphaël, both of whom were terrified of him. Jean Vanier had to ask him not to come back.

The poverty engendered by intellectual disabilities necessitated particular care. Those whose clouded spirits left them totally defenseless were truly the poorest of the poor. Many were treated as objects, like Philippe Seux, who had been dropped off one day at the care home without being informed that his mother, with whom he had been living, had died. Others were unable to understand why their bodies had betrayed them. Still others could not express what they were suffering or where they were hurting. They were unable to consciously process their own suffering. "A handicap is the most daunting of exclusions," writes Julia Kristeva in her book of correspondence with Jean Vanier.

BARELY NINE MONTHS after its founding, L'Arche absorbed Val Fleuri, and their boards of directors joined. L'Arche already consisted of more than fifty people, with two households. The essential components of a L'Arche community were in place: several small, family-style households; workplaces; and meeting spaces for celebrations. The project was growing, but did not yet have a well-defined identity when it came to faith. The community chapel was small, and there was no Catholic or Protestant church to attend in Trosly. "I was both director of an institution," writes Jean Vanier, "and shepherd of a little Christian community centered on poverty, but where many members either could not or would not profess to have a faith. How could unity be maintained in all that? That was the challenge."[18]

Fifty years later, this is still the challenge. There is a delicate articulation between the institutional and professional side of L'Arche, with its clear affiliation with the medical and social sector, and its two foundational features: Christianity and community. It has never been simply a question of caring for people with disabilities, but of living with them. No one wants to spend their whole life with "professionals," says Jean Vanier. Everyone wishes to live in a family or with friends, in community.

A Rift

THAT EVOLUTION TOWARD a specific structure was also the first crack in the relationship between Father Thomas and Jean Vanier, who did not see things eye to eye. "The conflict with Father Thomas was very painful," Jean recalls. The priest and the young man seemed to share the same theological and spiritual vision of a community founded on those who are the smallest and poorest. Yet Father Thomas could not conceive of not receiving every needy person. He had not realized that there were specific constraints associated with the needs of people with disabilities.

As L'Arche expanded and Jean's leadership role grew, the separation between the two men became even wider. Father Thomas could not follow what was moving Jean Vanier and L'Arche forward at full tilt. It was as though, for him, everything was moving too fast. This man who was so welcoming and open to others was clinging to a top-down model of the Catholic hierarchy, with a priest at the head. He could not understand why, when L'Arche communities were established in foreign countries, they should be ecumenical and even interreligious.

The Farm

IN 1971, WHEN L'ARCHE COMMUNITIES were already scattered throughout the world, one place in Trosly remained a particular place of welcome, a place to gather one's spirit and rest one's heart: the Farm. The Farm was a house of prayer, a spiritual center. It was a collection of buildings, low houses, gardens, and courtyards, with a large chapel, rooms for passing guests, a library, and, in the former sheep barn, an oratory where the Blessed Sacrament was displayed permanently. The oratory was a room with a low ceiling. In the middle was a wooden monstrance bearing the design of a cross and the silhouette of a person of which the face was the host. On the carpeted floor were several small rugs, a sheepskin, and a low armchair. It was a dim place, nestled in peace and silence. Everyone who needed a breather was welcome there.

Father Thomas, Jean Vanier, and others lectured and held retreats at the Farm. Father Thomas soaked up the suffering of others. He attracted all sorts of people. It seemed he didn't shield himself from anything, letting himself be silently devoured by waves of visitors, who often said that he "radiated the presence and love of God." The end of his life proved to be difficult, however. He who gave peace to those who came to him was often tomented and anguished. Exhausted and sick, Father Thomas left Trosly in January 1991 to go live with his brother. He died on February 4, 1993, and was buried near the chapel in Trosly.

THE STORY MIGHT HAVE ENDED HERE, but in June 2014 several shattering accounts brought to light disturbing revelations regarding Father Thomas's behavior during the years he spent at the Farm.[19] Beside the luminous figure of a suffering priest, there appeared the dark figure of a manipulator who used his psychological and spiritual influence to sexually exploit adult women – though not disabled people – under the cover of mystical experiences and personal blessings. Because Father Thomas is dead, it is not possible to initiate legal proceedings against him. But women came forward who wanted to be heard, and Jean Vanier wanted to hear them. A canonical inquest into the truth of the facts, presided over by Monsignor Pierre d'Ornellas, opened in December 2014 and was concluded the following April.

This was shocking and devastating for everyone, and a huge trauma for Jean Vanier. He could not believe it at first, but when the truth came out during the canonical inquest, he was overcome with a deep compassion for these abused women. In a public letter dated October 17, 2016, Jean unequivocally condemned Father Thomas's actions. He addressed the women directly: "I ask the forgiveness of the victims for not having measured soon enough the extent of their traumatization and for not having been sufficiently sensitive to their suffering."[20] He felt that Father Thomas, a man he had loved and admired, had profoundly betrayed his trust. Even while acknowledging the role of Father Thomas in his life, he had to undertake a harsh and difficult reinterpretation of their relationship.

L'Arche responded as an organization, too. In 2016, a listening point staffed by psychiatrists who were unaffiliated with L'Arche was established, open to anyone who wished to report that they had been abused by Father Thomas or any member of L'Arche. And on April 6, 2017, Jean joined the larger L'Arche community at the chapel in Trosly-Breuil for a Mass for the victims of Father Thomas. In the frank, forthright style characteristic of L'Arche, the celebrant, Monsignor d'Ornellas, acknowledged the tragedy, begged the victims' forgiveness, and prayed for the mission of L'Arche.

The Founding Pillars

L'ARCHE LEANS ON two apparently contradictory pillars: suffering and joy. We probably know that what is most visible is not necessarily what is most important. Next to those people whom history places in the limelight, there are many more in the background, weaving the secret threads that hold the tapestry together, like the thirty-six just men who, Hassidism says, are hidden away and holding up the world. In the same way, the story of L'Arche and Jean Vanier is woven on a framework of lives that are freely given, people who suffer in silence – the suffering of people with disabilities, their parents, and those who give their lives in service to them. Indeed, one of the pillars of L'Arche is suffering – the suffering of those with disabilities whom L'Arche receives, and the hidden suffering of those prayer warriors who offer their trials to God for L'Arche's mission.

The mystic Marthe Robin, founder of the Foyers de Charité, who was bedridden for fifty years, played an important role in the life of Jean Vanier. Jean attended Foyers de Charité retreats in Châteauneuf-de-Galaure, particularly in 1976 after a serious sickness left him bedridden for nearly two months. Marthe Robin also played an important role in the lives of numerous L'Arche assistants.

During his first conference in Montreal, Jean was surprised to learn that a woman named Rita had sent many people to hear him speak. But whoever was this Rita? Jean asked to meet her. She was a blind, paralyzed woman a bit older than he, who lived with her mother in a little house. In her physical suffering, she welcomed the many people who came to see her with overwhelming joy, treating each one as though they were the only person in the world she could have expected. "I told myself that that was the way God would welcome us,"[21] Jean Vanier recalls.

The second pillar of L'Arche is joy, a very special joy that is quite obvious, which visitors discover with awe in the L'Arche households. This joy has multiplied as L'Arche has expanded, much like the mustard seed Christ speaks of, which grows into a giant bush.[22]

Indeed, very early on, L'Arche was already spoken of in the plural. Around the first household and Val Fleuri, a whole movement was being created. The big, institutional dining hall in Val Fleuri was replaced with three smaller dining rooms, as well as a living room where residents could have a cup of coffee and pass an evening, and a garden where everyone was free to walk around. The number of households began to multiply, first in Trosly and then in the neighboring villages. It happened so quickly that in 1971 the residents of Trosly who had initially been either curious or delighted with the adventure were now worried that their village would be turned into a center for the intellectually disabled. They sent a petition to the local government. In their initial enthusiasm, the leaders of L'Arche had not taken into account the feelings of their neighbors. That was a mistake that has since been repaired, and it was actually a beneficial blunder in that it highlighted the importance of integrating the L'Arche communities into the social fabric of each locality. Jean Vanier discussed the problem with the local municipality, and they reached an agreement: future households would open in Cuise, Breuil, and Compiègne. Over the next ten years, fifteen new households welcomed more than one hundred and fifty people – most of them coming from the nearby psychiatric hospital in Clermont.

Trosly, with its ten L'Arche households and the Farm, became the "motherhouse of L'Arche for the reception and training of a great number of assistants who, in turn, were able to leave for other communities in France and in other parts of the world."[23] These were students and young professionals – mostly Canadians at first, but later Americans, French, Germans, Indians, and Japanese – who came to observe, stayed for some time, then either left or decided to spend their life in Trosly. Some later founded new communities in other parts of the world, and in this way L'Arche was transformed into an international movement. In order for there to be a L'Arche, says Jean Vanier, it is not enough to have money. First and foremost, there must be committed people.

5

Guide

IN TROSLY, THE LITTLE TRIO of Jean, Philippe, and Raphaël had attracted visitors from the very beginning. It was Jean Vanier, in large part, who found such committed people – perhaps "sparked their vocations" would be a better expression. People from the village and friends of Jean, but also foreigners, came spontaneously to volunteer, and then committed themselves to the work. They were captivated by this new style of community life, as well as by the aura surrounding its founder. They came to hear Jean Vanier's commentary on the Gospels in the first household in 1964, when he gave his first talks in Toronto in 1965, and when he preached his first retreat at Marylake Monastery in Canada in 1968. More and more people came to listen to him, and soon he was being invited to speak all over the world, and wrote the first in a long series of books. Jean seemed to be setting quite another story in motion: in addition to being the founder, he was becoming a spiritual guide.

On a personal level, the years following the founding of L'Arche were difficult. Georges Vanier died on March 5, 1967, in Rideau Hall, the governor general's residence in Ottawa. He died with the same courage and humor he had shown all his life. Jean Vanier was able to be near his father during those last days. "Toward the end of the afternoon, one of his aide-de-camps came into the room and, seeing the oxygen mask affixed to his face, said to him, 'One would think you just arrived from outer space.' 'No,' he replied, without blinking, 'I'm just about to go there.'"[1]

Jean's grandmother, Thérèse de Salaberry, stayed in Paris after her daughter Pauline returned to Canada. She was living in a hotel. Jean came to see her regularly and took care of her. In 1968, he learned that her mind was slipping and she roamed the corridors at night. She had money, so with it he bought her Les Marronniers, a large dilapidated house in Trosly, and had it remodeled. In order to keep her from being disoriented – she was nearly ninety-five years old – he had the bathroom remodeled so that it was identical to the pink and black one in her former home. Unfortunately, she died on February 28, 1969, the very morning he came to get her.

His mother, Pauline, had been concerned when, instead of teaching philosophy, Jean chose to settle in Trosly. She was down-right shocked by the living conditions in the little L'Arche house, so she considered giving Les Marronniers to the community. She returned to Canada, and in 1971 she attended a retreat at the Carmel in Montreal. On the last day, the Gospel reading for the Mass was the story of the rich young man, whom Jesus asked to sell all he had and follow him. She started weeping. It was she, in turn, who decided to sell everything. She left to settle in Trosly at Les Marronniers – the house that had been bought for her mother.

Pauline lived there for the next twenty years, welcoming, like a grandmother to everyone, both people with disabilities and assistants. The Chatelaine of Rideau Hall became Granny Vanier. On Sundays, when Jean was there – and he was never there enough for his liking – people would congregate in the living room. Crowned with white hair, staring ahead – she was going blind little by little – she sat on a red velvet chair. Her son folded up his great height and sat on a small wicker chair, with a Bible open on his knees, and commented on a Gospel passage. Young people, people with disabilities, and guests were seated here and there, some on the floor, others in wheelchairs or on chairs. They listened. The silence was broken from time to time when a person with disabilities laughed, moaned, or stood up.

Leader, Friend, Brother

JEAN VANIER'S APPEARANCE does not leave people indifferent. He is tall – six foot six – and very thin, with an ascetic face. He has white hair – it was black, once – blue eyes, a smile, and a radiant expression. He has an air of tranquil strength that attracts and reassures people. "He is an alluring person in the true sense of the term: someone who leads you out of yourself,"[2] remarks Françoise Laroudie, Secretary General of L'Arche in France. She remembers her first meeting with him in the magnificent Paribas hall where she dealt with mergers and acquisitions. One of her clients wanted to make a donation and someone mentioned L'Arche. François introduced the potential donor to Jean. She was struck by his soft, intense expression. His lively intelligence, coupled with a palpable quality of presence and empathy, beguiled her. He was there – really present.

He has that capacity of being completely in tune with those around him, of gazing candidly at those to whom he is speaking. And yet he gives the impression that he comes from a different world. Around the table at Val Fleuri on a March day in 2014, fifty years after the founding of L'Arche, young assistants, like their predecessors of bygone days, find it difficult to verbalize their impressions of Jean. "He really looks. How can I express it? When he looks at you, it's like an appeal, an invitation." In any case, one of them declares that when he first met Jean Vanier, "in an instant I better understood why Zacchaeus came down from the tree!" Another one, less religious but just as clear, says, "Jean Vanier – but he is Alice's rabbit!" Alice's rabbit? "But of course. The rabbit. The one who led Alice into Wonderland, right?"

What is most surprising about Jean is his capacity to embody qualities that seem contradictory. He is physically imposing, but striking in his simplicity. He has a lively spirit and seems to understand what someone is saying before they finish speaking, but he never monopolizes the conversation, and creates a space where each person can express himself or herself. His schedule is always full, but he gives the impression to his guests, or even the stranger he meets on the train platform, of having all the time in the world. He knows many people, but treats each new acquaintance with delight. He is confident and, without being naïve, he believes in signs of providence. He is open but enigmatic, rooted but free, pragmatic but mystical. He has a sense of humor. He recalls the time he embarked on an interminable train ride to Bangalore, on a visit to India. Invited to share provisions with some of the Indian travelers, he discovered that all he had to offer them was Laughing Cow cheese!

People often follow a spiritual master because of his charismatic appeal. Jean Vanier unquestionably has such charisma. He attracts. He charms. He convinces. The dangers that surround the person who possesses these strange powers are well known. But Jean Vanier is just as concerned with the freedom of others as with his own freedom. And for him, the spiritual guide is first of all someone who helps others continue on the path of inner freedom.

He is neither priest, nor psychologist, nor therapist. He considers himself to be simply a fellow traveler who walks with others and helps them along their own paths. Talking with the L'Arche assistants today, it is striking that it seems everyone quickly forgets that he is the founder, and instead feels that he is their friend. That is the word that most often comes to mind when assistants, old or new, are asked who Jean Vanier is for them. A father? A grandfather, even, for these young people in their twenties? The founder? "Well, no," they say, "Jean Vanier is a friend." In the beginning they are afraid they will be intimidated. After all, he's the founder! But then, he is so easygoing . . . And for the disabled people who are welcomed into the community, who is he? He's a friend to you, too? "Oh, no," Simone answers as she hides her paralyzed arm under the table and speaks with difficulty. "No, he's not a friend. He's a brother."

The Guide

RIGHT FROM THE BEGINNING of L'Arche, Jean Vanier took on the role of spiritual guide in addition to that of founder and organizer. He was a guide not only for the assistants but for many other people as well: people in search of meaning and people who, upon meeting him, suddenly discovered an inner thirst for something they hadn't heretofore known. This was what had been, along with prayer, the beginning and end of his action during so many years. And this is what remains for him today, since he has pulled back from his travels. For him, to guide is first of all to listen. And so, in his office, or wherever he is, Jean Vanier listens – several hours each day, bent a bit forward, absolutely attentive, completely absorbed by what is being said as well as what is left unsaid. He listens to the assistants, but also to the young woman who doesn't quite know what to do with her life, to the man destroyed by alcohol, and to the parents who have been shattered by their child's disability. He listens to the priest who doesn't have the courage to go on, to the disabled woman who is so angry with her sister who never comes to see her, and to the man who wants to abandon his family. He listens to the misfortunes, the dramas, the dashed hopes, the pain, the confusion, the dreams, the joys, the achievements. His door is always open. He understands.

He inspires trust in other people. In his presence, people let down their masks and speak the truth. They hear themselves say things they would never have dared to admit before. He speaks but little, and the few words he does speak reach the heart of the person he's with. Those who meet him leave in peace. "How do you translate the essence of that man who is, both literally and figuratively, a giant – a being who connects directly and without airs, touching each one of us in our most vulnerable spot with openness and compassion?" writes the Canadian physician, Martha Bala, mother of four children. Martha lived in Trosly, then in a L'Arche community in India, before becoming a member of the board of directors of L'Arche International. "How is it that people of all ages, colors, cultures, origins, nationalities, and beliefs are touched by him, attracted to him, feel understood by him, feel close to him?

"Jean Vanier speaks to people's hearts, drawing out all the hardness with tenderness and humility. His capacity to empathize with that wound that each person secretly carries in himself or herself is the fruit of a life entirely given over to faithful prayer. The hours of attentive and patient listening have continued to sharpen this gift – this ability to hear the cry of those who are rejected and without a voice, the life of deep pain of so many people, the aspirations of his own heart, and the tenderness of Jesus, who is his source of inspiration."[3]

Jean has a profound intuition of human beings and of their beauty. "They don't realize that they are so beautiful!" he says. "They are so crushed with guilt and feel very dirty. They don't have any self-confidence. They do not realize that they are loved. They don't know how valuable and how precious they are."[4] He claims that the only thing he does is joyfully welcome them, look upon them with tenderness, and show them trust. Because, according to him, there is no human growth without that relationship as the basis, that relationship that says, "I love you just as you are."

The great king Solomon asked God for "a listening heart."[5] That is also the gift that Jean Vanier received, and that is what he wishes to give to those who come to meet with him. Not that they have a lot to listen to: he offers little or no advice. But in a few words, he opens doors that had previously seemed closed, giving people the courage to express hidden desires and fears.

Friends of Jean Vanier say that he seems to have the ability to speak just the right word, have just the right gesture, or make the right decision. Has he ever been wrong? Yes, of course. But he

knows how to wait, to analyze, and then to act. It is as though
he were following a different internal guide and seeing things in
a different way. He says he waits for signs, that he has deep inner
convictions. He doesn't seem to go about a project according to the
normal course of action. If he did, he never would have launched
L'Arche! Neither does he seem to be constrained by ordinary
social conventions. He is liable to stop abruptly in the street to
talk with someone, as though that were the most important thing
he had to do, even though he is late and people are waiting for him.
Jean once got into an animated discussion with a very surprised
backpacker, who was only asking for some money (which he got,
by the way), but who ended up opening up his heart to him. Jean is
also able to suspend the well-cultivated manner of his upbringing
in favor of surprising displays of love. One day, he had an audience with the pope along with other community founders. Each
person bowed with deference before the pontiff. But Jean Vanier
threw himself on his knees and kissed him. And, when he was
invited to have breakfast with Pope John Paul II after morning
Mass, he declared, impulsively, "Your Holiness, I dream all the
time about you. If I dream about you, you must be my father! And
if you are my father, I need to see you from time to time!" Who
would speak so freely and directly?

"He seems to be guided by the Holy Spirit," says Odile Ceyrac.

"God dwells in him and leads him," says Nadine Tokar, the
founder of the L'Arche community in Honduras.

"He has a companionship with Jesus that I find to be absolutely
extraordinary. He has founded his life on Christ. And Christ is his
friend and his Lord," says Gérard Daucourt, the Bishop of Nanterre.

So many different expressions that say the same thing: his standards, the things that motivate him, and his views of others seem
to come from elsewhere. Jean recognizes that what he wants, first of
all, is to follow Jesus. He founded his life on this promise from the
Gospel of John: "If you remain in my word, then you are truly my
disciples. You shall know the truth, and the truth shall set you free."[6]

The Preacher

WHEN JEAN VANIER took a position at the University of Toronto, he discovered that he had a "gift for speaking." Even so, his first lectures were not brilliant. The students didn't seem to be interested in his classes and, to his great consternation, the young professor of ethics watched the classrooms empty out as he followed his fixed lesson plan on the topic of justice. But the rooms filled up, and even seemed too small, when he began to talk about love, friendship, and sexuality. His lectures were so crowded that he was finally offered the use of a large auditorium, which also proved insufficient. The success of his first speeches in 1965, also in Toronto, prompted other universities to invite him. Jean was surprised at the effect of his words. He wasn't saying anything new, only elaborating on the Gospels. But what he said touched people, moved them, and gave them confidence. For the person who heard Jean's message – "Fear not!" – the world opened up and things became possible. No one was a prisoner of his or her past or complexes, fears, or remorse. No one was condemned. Life was an adventure that had to be lived. To live, Jean affirmed, was to go freely forward under the loving eye of a God who rejoices at each step of our progress toward holiness, toward the joy of being ourselves.

IN 1968, THE DIOCESE of Toronto asked Jean Vanier to host a retreat for priests at Marylake. He was surprised: a layman hosting a retreat for priests? Jean remarked later, laughing, that his surprise showed his naïveté. Being very busy with L'Arche, he hadn't really been aware of the stir that was fomented by the Second Vatican Council in the Catholic Church, especially in Canada and France.

After hesitating for a long time, Jean agreed to accept the invitation, on several conditions. It would be a week-long, silent retreat that gathered together priests, members of religious orders, and lay people. He asked Father O'Connor, whom he had known at Eau Vive, and who was very much involved in the Charismatic

Renewal Movement, to come help him. Jean carefully prepared what he was going to say in the silence of the Carmel of Cognac, but he was seriously intimidated when, before his audience, he was introduced with the title of "preacher." He spoke easily and freely, however, and was encouraged by the enthusiasm of those who were listening to him. Father O'Connor's evening prayers were, some said, lifeless in comparison. Yet Father O'Connor and Jean Vanier understood that the heart of the retreat was taking place not in their words but in times of silent prayer.

There were sixty participants at that first retreat in the Marylake convent, sixty people who, comforted and galvanized, decided to launch a similar retreat in another town. Thus, the Faith and Sharing Federation was born. Like a baton that is passed, the retreats succeeded one another – each little group of organizers passed the organization on to future organizers: in Canada, the United States, Great Britain, and South America. Soon it was no longer sixty people attending the retreat, but five hundred people in Seattle, and then, in Chile, twenty-two hundred.

In France and Canada in the early seventies, Jean Vanier also launched Katimavik, an organization aimed at young adults who would normally flee from the word "retreat." (In the Inuit culture, a *katimavik* is a communal room.) The organization, which promoted living together in order to "meet Jesus,"[7] eventually spread throughout the world, and Jean Vanier used it as a platform for two- and three-day retreats for people with disabilities, assistants, and young people.

Everywhere Jean went, he asked that these retreats be open places that would bring together religious and lay people, disabled and healthy, patients and chaplains, parishioners and clerics, students and educators. He was committed to breaking down barriers between factions and insular groups. He even succeeded in organizing a retreat for prison guards, directors, and ex-prisoners, where participants were not supposed to know who was who.

WHEN PREACHING AT A RETREAT, Jean Vanier typically
entered the gathering discreetly, during the singing of a prayer, for
example. He sat on a low chair, whether in front of forty people at
the Farm, in a prison visiting room, or before hundreds of people
in the packed basilica of Notre-Dame-des-Victoires. He placed a
little table next to him holding an icon, a lit candle, and a bouquet
of flowers. He held a Bible in his hand and laid his notes on the
table, but he didn't look at them. He spoke softly and clearly; there
was sometimes a hint of a laugh on his lips. His train of thought
was clear and articulate. Listeners found him easy to understand,
and they discovered anew things they thought they had known.
His words carved out a silent space in each person, a place where
tired and unheeded phrases took on meaning once again. His tone
and delivery, the rhythm of his sentences, and the ebb and flow of
his arguments, returning again and again to certain themes like a
refrain, created a sort of unity within the audience. Each listener
felt both unique, as though Jean were speaking directly to him
or her, and united to the others – both those in the room and
the people from the Bible and L'Arche about whom Jean spoke.
Indeed, these people seemed to be there in the room too: Jesus, of
course, the intimate friend and companion, washing his disciples'
feet or sitting, tired, at the edge of the well, the Samaritan woman
and her impudence and great suffering; his L'Arche companions
Philippe and Raphaël; or Claudia, Eric, and Patrick.

When giving an address to large crowds – such as the five
hundred at the Mutualité, or the one thousand five hundred in
the great hall of UNESCO in Paris – Jean Vanier spoke standing
up. He gestured more emphatically and his voice was louder, his
tone vibrant and confident. His remarks were firm, and yet there
was nothing of the severe rhetorician about him. In speaking, Jean
had nothing to sell: he was not seeking acclaim or approval, and
the crowd felt this. The story he told concerned everyone, and he
narrated it to the disarmed conscience of his listeners.

"I am not trying to prove anything," Jean says of his speaking, "nor to show that I am right or that I am knowledgeable."[8] He simply says what he believes. For example, he did not mince his words when he reminded everyone at the 2008 Quebec Eucharistic Congress that, in Christianity, the good news announced to the poor is not just good words. It is not just about saying "Jesus loves you" to the poor person lying on the sidewalk. Rather, one should say, "I love you, and I want to enter into a relationship with you" – and then stay. How did he manage to combine demands and tenderness, understanding and clarity, the absolute certainty of what he believes and absolute respect for what others believe? Jean Cocteau, a French author, writes, "We must close the eyes of the dead with gentleness; but we must also open the eyes of the living with gentleness." Jean Vanier opened the eyes of those who heard him with gentleness – but he opened them.

Between sessions at his retreats, Jean welcomed participants who requested to see him – a quarter of an hour each on average. Without wasting time, he got straight to the essentials. Sometimes a simple phrase sufficed. At the end of one retreat, a young woman approached him, smiling: "Can I show you a picture of Julie?" she said. "Take a look. Do you remember what you told me twelve years ago? Do you remember? I was lost, really lost. I was pregnant. I was told that the child had Down syndrome. I was torn up. On one hand, I was told to get an abortion. On the other hand, I was told I shouldn't. They all said I would regret having done it or not having done it. I talked to you about it as I was leaving a conference, like the one today. You told me, 'Have the baby and give it to me.' It made my blood boil! I said to myself, 'He's crazy; how could I give him my baby?' I was appalled. But at that moment, she became my baby and no longer a problem to be solved."

"I didn't have the chance to meet with him often," says a man in his fifties today. "Two or three times, maybe, but I remember. One day, when I was twenty years old, he asked me, 'Do you pray?' 'But I don't believe in God,' I told him. 'Never mind, pray anyway!'

And ever since then I have prayed – to what, to whom? I don't know – but I pray each morning."

The Teacher

JEAN'S MESSAGE RANG TRUE, not only in his meetings and retreats, but also in his writings. He wrote constantly – in airports, in train stations, at night when he couldn't sleep because of jetlag. He covered notebooks with his small, blue – he only uses blue ink – handwriting. Nowadays, he writes at the Orval Monastery, where he spends the month of August, and in his house in Trosly, after all the visitors have left.

He often sent notes on postcards simply to support, console, or greet the many people he had encountered. He also wrote the long newsletters that have been indispensable since the beginning of L'Arche. The first of these was published barely three weeks after moving in. At that time he clarified his objectives for the community: "As you know, L'Arche wants to create an authentic spiritual family, a network of friendship and brotherhood dedicated to the poor of our society, to helping the physically and intellectually disabled. L'Arche is not uniquely the work of a little group of people. If we have been able to move quickly into Trosly, it is due to the generosity of numerous friends. These newsletters will keep you up to date on the activities and progress of L'Arche. They will also help us clarify our common ideal and to stimulate our love for the poor, who are, in a special way, the face of Jesus."[9]

Jean wrote books too, more than thirty of them: collections of talks, retreats, and radio and TV broadcasts, some of which are rather short, such as *Finding Peace, Encountering 'the Other,'* and *From Brokenness to Community*; others longer, such as *Befriending the Stranger*. Then there are essays: *Community and Growth*, on community life; *Man and Woman God Made Them*, on male-female relationships and sexuality; *Becoming Human*, on humanity and anthropology; *Signs of the Times*, on the philosophy of L'Arche; and *Made for Happiness*, the publication of his philosophy dissertation. He also wrote more meditative works such as *The Broken Body, Seeing Beyond Depression, Tears of Silence, Drawn into the Mystery of Jesus through the Gospel of John*, and *Jesus, the Gift of Love*. Then there are books about L'Arche's history and spirituality, such as *The Heart of L'Arche*, and a collection of letters from L'Arche, *Our Life Together: A Memoir in Letters*.

As with his spoken word, the simplicity and clarity of his writings are striking. People for whom obscurity goes hand in hand with profundity might find him simplistic, but they would be wrong. The reader does not require any particular knowledge, but he or she must learn to let go, to be guided, to follow the twists and turns and detours of Jean's way of thinking, which weaves three different threads together: the Gospels, people's stories, and the light shed on them by philosophy, psychology, and the other social sciences. His thoughts do not resemble the clean contours of a French garden, in which the arrangement of the flower beds is itself an integral part of the garden's beauty. They are more like an English garden, where the rigor of the construction is concealed by meandering paths through abundant flowerbeds.

Jean's writing style owes much to his upbringing in England, but it also owes a lot to pragmatism. It is not a question of the power of his intellect, but of being able to find the right words to convey his knowledge and understanding, and also his deepest emotions and life experiences. Rather than simply making the reader understand, he draws them into an experience, so that often his writing takes on the feeling of a poem, without exactly being one. The tempo of the reading contributes to its meaning. "God leads so gently, so slowly," writes Jean Vanier, "and so our hearts become peaceful."

There are words that can only be heard with a peaceful heart. That peaceful pace is evident in his written work, which leads readers gently toward a new understanding of the world and of themselves. His writings do not foster an intellectual reading that would allow us to distance ourselves from the message conveyed. The things of which Jean Vanier speaks and writes, these "things hidden since the creation of the world,"[10] touch the reader's inner experience.

THE GOSPEL JEAN IS TALKING ABOUT really is good news, and he repeats it untiringly. "I've come to announce some very good news – the news of God's nearness," he said in January 2014 at UNESCO. "God is near to each one of us – a loving nearness." The gospel is never a moral question for him, or a question of rites or theoretical knowledge. It is rather a story of an encounter with a God who people need no longer fear, a God who, in order to show us who he is, made himself man in Jesus – a gentle, tender Jesus who stands humbly at the door, as the Book of Revelation says, and waits for us to invite him to enter. He is a God who washes the feet of his disciples and begs them to let themselves be loved and healed.

We have a God incarnate, whom we do not need to look for in some inaccessible place. He is a fellow traveler and guide who leads us into the mystery of life, allowing us to truly live and to see him as he really is. "What is truth?" Pilate asked Christ. Yes, what is truth? It is reality, Jean Vanier writes in *Drawn into the Mystery of Jesus through the Gospel of John*, that reality that scares us so much and is so often hidden behind the fog of our illusions and desires. This is the truth that we neither create nor possess, and that we cannot simply discover through science, but which reveals itself in the journey we take with him who said, "I am the way, the truth, and the light."

> The light of truth, then, is the gentle marriage
> of what we see and experience,
> with what we have received from above and the Word of God,

each one enlightening the other, each one calling us to live in God
and to see things through the loving eyes and loving heart of God.[11]

Seeing things through God's eyes brings gentleness and beauty
to the world. The God Jean Vanier preaches is also a tender and
liberating God. Far from confining us in commandments and
prohibitions that hinder us from living, he wrests us from the
slavery of fear and leads us to peace. Thus Jean Vanier continues:

> Slaves are never free. They cannot be at peace
> in the "home" of their own body,
> in the "home" of reality, or in the "home" of God.
> They are always on the run, consumed by anguish,
> running from reality, from what *is*
> into a world of illusion.
> Only the Son can liberate us from slavery
> and bring us into our real home: the home of God.[12]

Jean Vanier's influence grew as the number of L'Arche communities in the world grew. When he left the navy, he had renounced
faraway seas and lands. But since founding L'Arche, he has traveled
to more places than most sailors! He had been a professor, but as
founder of L'Arche he has hosted retreats and conferences, and
given lectures to more people than almost any university professor!
He had renounced the priesthood, but he has become a spiritual
guide to more disciples than most priests! Jean Vanier's story is the
realization of the promise in the Gospels: "Truly I tell you . . . no
one who has left home or brothers or sisters or mother or father
or children or fields for me and the gospel will fail to receive a
hundred times as much in this present age."[13]

The man who finally found his homeland in Trosly-Breuil
roamed the world. What with retreats, speeches, community visits,
and participation in various federations and international councils,
during nearly forty years he traveled more than six months out of
every year. The international expansion of L'Arche, the founding

of Faith and Light in 1971, and the organization he put in place to ensure the unity of such diverse communities compelled him to take up the pilgrim's staff and wander across the world.

6

Pilgrim

THE INTERNATIONAL GROWTH of L'Arche, beginning in 1969 with the first foreign community – Daybreak, founded in Canada – was impressive. Forty-six communities in fourteen countries were founded in the seventies: five in France, fourteen in Canada, four in India, four in Belgium, five in the United States, five in Great Britain, two in Honduras, and one each in Haiti, Ireland, Burkina Faso, the Ivory Coast, Japan, Denmark, and Australia. The forty-three communities founded in the eighties added to L'Arche's geographical spread: Spain, Italy, Switzerland, the Dominican Republic, Mexico, Brazil, Germany, the Philippines, and Poland. The nineties, with sixteen new communities, saw the addition of Slovenia, Austria, Syria, Uganda, Zimbabwe, and the Netherlands. Twenty-five communities were established from 2000 to 2013 in Egypt, the Palestinian territories, Ukraine, Bangladesh, Korea, Croatia, and Argentina.

Curious founder, curious foundations. Despite its success, Jean does not cling to ownership of the organization he began. Alain Saint Macary relates how, as a young assistant, he was shocked to hear Jean Vanier praising L'Arche in front of some of the assistants. "I said to myself, he lacks a little modesty, since he is the one who founded it," he recalls. "But then I understood. He was enthralled, because he felt that he was only an instrument, and that he had only put himself at the service of a venture that was higher than he was. It wasn't his venture, but God's."[1] L'Arche was God's project, for Jean and for the committed assistants at his side. But this rapid growth can also be explained by other factors.

France and other wealthy countries found themselves in desperate need of structures for people with disabilities. The government was ready to finance the daily costs of patient care, as well as innovative projects. In Western countries, a new understanding of mental illness and psychiatry was emerging in the sixties, and specialists explored new ways to care for people besides placing them in asylums. This new interpretation of mental illness was at the same time political, sociological, and psychoanalytical; it could almost be called anti-psychiatry.

There was also a general societal movement of people in search of new values and new ways of living. Baby boomers were coming of age during the sixties, and they wanted to find a way to live that was different from their parents. The hippie movement was spreading the watchwords of peace, love, and communal living, and promoting a return to the simplicity of nature. In the Catholic Church, the Second Vatican Council, convened from 1962 to 1965, opened doors; the Charismatic Renewal at the end of the sixties opened others. This served to rattle some and enthuse others. It was an era characterized by invention and generosity. All sorts of communities were born all over the world. The growth of L'Arche was likely due to this general movement as much as to the charismatic personality of Jean Vanier. Still, the history of L'Arche is inseparable from the meetings and retreats he led, for his fervent enthusiasm drew people in increasing numbers.

Ecumenical Communities

MOST OF THE EARLY L'Arche communities in North America were born in the wake of Faith and Sharing Federation retreats, which were held in many places across Canada and the United

States. The words of Jean Vanier reached the hearts of Anglicans, Evangelicals, and other Protestants, who began to live together in these ecumenical communities.

Jean Vanier has always said that the ecumenical and interreligious dimensions of L'Arche were not planned. They flowed not from specific schemes, nor from the Second Vatican Council, but from pure pragmatism. In Jean's view, each community was naturally rooted in the culture and religion of the people with disabilities it welcomed. That pragmatic embrace of religious diversity was confusing to some in the Catholic Church, who had a hard time classifying Jean's work in one or another category. Still, it is easy to imagine that Jean Vanier's immersion as a young boy in the Anglican atmosphere at Dartmouth Naval College, as well as the religion of his beloved Scottish nanny, played an important role in his spiritual openmindedness and his capacity to accept the fact that L'Arche was sailing into the unknown waters of ecumenism.

Indeed, it was out of the question for Jean Vanier to try to convert anyone or impose a faith. "The L'Arche communities want to encourage each person to grow in the life of faith he has received from his family, and to integrate into their own religious traditions," he wrote in 1995. But this does not mean falling into some vague religious syncretism: "L'Arche does not want to create a new church with its own rules, services, and liturgy. We want to humbly walk with the various denominations in their thirst for unity, with all their imperfections, theological differences, and rules (particularly those about sharing communion). L'Arche recognizes everything that unites the disciples of Jesus."[2] Jean's sister, Thérèse, was instrumental in taking L'Arche's ecumenism from a theoretical level to a practical one. After studying in England to become a hematologist, she founded the Barfrestone L'Arche in 1974, firmly planted in the heart of Anglicanism, about nine miles from Canterbury. Anglican theologians such as David Ford, head of theological studies at Cambridge, and Frances Young regularly worked with her on the theme of ecumenism.

In the meantime, people were learning to live together harmoniously, adhering to their religious affiliations and personal convictions without letting them become reasons for discord. They learned to tolerate the tensions, sometimes created by individual differences, without relegating the religious dimension to the private sphere or avoiding differences in a sort of artificial unity. It was necessary to continually refocus on what people shared in common, particularly one conviction that contributed to the deep unity of the L'Arche communities – a conviction that, in addition to the sacraments of each faith tradition, there existed what Jean Vanier called the "sacrament of the poor." He writes in *A Door of Hope*, "In the act of loving and welcoming the poor, with gestures of love and openness, of tenderness and firmness, God is silently present. The heart of the poor is also a sacrament,"[3] that is to say, a dwelling place of the presence of God. For Jean Vanier, the path to unity between peoples and religions passes through receiving the poor, who represent Jesus, who in turn represents the Father. If the Father "is hidden in the beauties of creation, in the splendor of the liturgies, and in the wisdom of the theologians and scholars, he is also hidden in the broken body of the lepers and the sick, of those who suffer."[4]

India

THE SECOND L'ARCHE COMMUNITY outside of France opened in India in 1970, meaning L'Arche was now not only ecumenical, but interreligious. A concurrence of events and improbable encounters led to its creation, and Jean Vanier discovered both a country that moved him deeply and a spiritual master who made a lasting impression on him.

L'Arche in India – what an idea! It was a country to which Jean had never traveled and that had not particularly interested him. But one day in 1969, he received a letter from a Major Ramachandra, a disciple of Mahatma Gandhi, asking him to do something for people with intellectual disabilities in India. At the same time, the father of Mira Ziaudinn, a young Indian Catholic, fell sick. Mira, who had come to live in Trosly in 1965, was the daughter of a Muslim and a Hindu. She felt the need to go care for her father, but she agonized at the thought of leaving L'Arche. What could she do? Create a L'Arche community in her country? Gabrielle Einsle, a young German woman living in Montreal, was ready to help her. They spoke to Jean, who listened but didn't know how to accomplish this any better than they did.

In February, he met Lester Pearson, the head of the Canadian International Development Agency, an organization charged with financing projects in the developing world. Jean spoke to him about India. Pearson was in agreement, but he wanted to see a plan and a budget. No problem! Without knowing anything about the country, Jean and Gabrielle drafted both documents right then and there. The project was accepted, and the money arrived. Gabrielle and Mira flew to Bangalore in September, and Jean followed a month later. The day after his arrival, he met with Major Ramachandra. The major had come to offer a house. And so, Asha Niketan, "The Dwelling Place of Hope," was born. The board of directors and the budding community brought together Hindus, Muslims, and Christians in the first interreligious L'Arche community. Three more interreligious communities would follow in India: one in Calcutta in 1972; another in Madras in 1975; and a third in Calicut, Kerala in 1977. Other interreligious L'Arche communities later formed in Bangladesh and in the West Bank.

FOR JEAN, INDIA was overwhelming. Together with Mother Teresa and Father Ceyrac, a French Jesuit, he visited hospices, leprosariums, hospitals, and shanty towns. He was at the same time horrified and filled with wonder. Amid the poverty, something radiated – something that moved him and gave him pause. "Calcutta is a town of misery and death," he wrote in 1972.

"Sickness, filth, stench, stagnant water, dead rats, and naked children who sleep on the sidewalks are everywhere! And yet there is such a tenderness: faces shining with beauty; the marvelous eyes of the children; wise, aged white-bearded faces; young girls with clear, candid eyes; young people who laugh; people who help one another; and swarms of people milling about the streets. It was a confused world, and yet I felt there was hope! I felt at home, happy to be there, happy to be in the streets, to watch the people and to travel about in the crowded buses. There was a great peace in my heart, a peace I had rarely experienced. It's hard to explain. I was discovering the beauty of Calcutta, the beauty of the poor."[5]

With so many people sleeping in the streets and so many children dying of hunger, the lot of people with disabilities was even worse than in other places, Jean realized. He saw hundreds of naked men and women locked in cages in psychiatric hospitals. In light of suffering of this magnitude, to many it would seem ridiculous to open a little house in a garden where only a tiny number of people would live.

Nevertheless, as soon as he arrived in Bangalore, Jean rolled up his sleeves. He cleared the land, played soccer with community members, did the cooking, washed dishes, and asked himself what kind of prayer life people like Gurunathan, who was from an orthodox Hindu family, and Joseph, a Catholic, could have together. They spoke little, and what they said was in the Tamil language. And yet, life together evolved, Indian style. Everyone ate sitting on the ground and slept on mats. They gathered for evening prayer in a small room where Joseph sang snippets of hymns and Gurunathan, who had placed before him an image of his god, bowed down and kissed the ground.

IT WAS IN BANGALORE, in the far recesses of a little bookstore, that Jean Vanier found the works of Mahatma Gandhi, who would become another of his spiritual guides. He still has those books in his home, little yellowed books with paper that is lightly pockmarked with moldy spots. "Meeting the spirit and thought of Gandhi, seeing his life of prayer and his love for all people – especially outcasts – profoundly changed my heart. I experienced a true conversion,"[6] he writes in the preface to *Never Again Alone*. Of course, Jean was cognizant of Gandhi's doctrine of nonviolence and its political outcomes. He was impressed with his work on behalf of the untouchables. He was touched by his lifestyle in community, where he chose the humblest tasks – Gandhi was the one who cleaned the toilets at the ashram. But Jean Vanier was especially moved to learn about the suffering and humiliation that was, in a certain sense, at the root of everything. He is still moved by the image of Gandhi as a young Indian lawyer surrounded by his baggage, sitting on the ground in South Africa after being ejected from a first-class train car because he was an Indian, despite having paid for his ticket. The emotion in his voice is palpable when he talks about it. What should one who is humiliated do? Humiliate others in turn? Flee? Find a new way?

He is still moved by the way Gandhi committed himself, from that day onward, to the long combat that eventually resulted in the recognition of civil rights for Indians in South Africa and the independence of the Indian nation. He is also moved by the example of Martin Luther King Jr., who won the Nobel Peace Prize in 1964, the same year L'Arche was founded, and who knew the humiliation of segregation from the time he was just six years old, when he was forbidden to play with two white boys. He is moved by the example of Francis of Assisi who, seeking the glory of war, instead experienced the humiliations of prison in Perouse, sickness, depression, and a breakdown in which he languished for almost two years before picking himself up again. Jean Vanier says that "there is a connection between these three stories and L'Arche," and he does not feel it was by chance that L'Arche federation conferences were held in Assisi, Saint Francis's town; in Calcutta, Gandhi's town; and in Atlanta, Martin Luther King Jr.'s town.

RENÉ LEROY, ONE OF THE PEOPLE with disabilities who joined L'Arche in 1978, says, "I think that Jean Vanier is unhappy when he sees people suffer."[7] The suffering he is able to put up with the least, the suffering that, in the words of René, makes him most unhappy, is humiliation. Jean fears this for himself, too. "My biggest fear," he says, "is to be humiliated."[8]

Jean says that buried deep within each of us is the memory of a time of humiliation and rejection, a fragile point from which anguish is born. We strive to conceal this moment, persistently hiding from it in order to survive. Perhaps for Jean, that point was when his sick mother was no longer able to care for him, or when he was sent away from Eau Vive. Today, a paradox troubles him: he is praised and honored because he lives with people who have been humiliated, instead of being humiliated with them.

He often says that people with intellectual disabilities are the most humiliated people on earth. He has dedicated his life to those who are of no account, those whom the world considers to have no usefulness or value, who are shut away far from public view and are sometimes even denied the status of human beings. He tries in every way to restore their dignity and honor them, to put into practice the words of Saint Paul: "On the contrary, those parts of the body that seem to be weaker are indispensable, and the parts that we think are less honorable we treat with special honor."[9] L'Arche came into being in order to surround those who are considered the least honorable with honor. Faith and Light, another organization Jean Vanier helped found, has a similar goal.

Faith and Light

JEAN VANIER loves pilgrimages. "We are all pilgrims," he once said. "In our hearts, we never settle down, and that is why we suffer from anxiety. The external pilgrimage is a sign of the inner pilgrimage, where we are all in search of that place inside ourselves, in the profoundest recesses of our being, where there is deep peace."[10]

That first summer at L'Arche, Jean headed off for Lourdes, along with Philippe, Raphaël, several friends, and a few residents of Val Fleuri. The Cité Secours offered them room and board, friends loaned cars or offered to drive, and the little convoy – thirty people in all – hit the road. Jean Vanier was struck by the effects of that first pilgrimage: "The fact of traveling together, undertaking long walks, living outside their familiar surroundings in conditions that were precarious, brought us into brotherly unity," he wrote in 1978. He also discovered that the pilgrims with intellectual disabilities were deeply sensitive to the symbols of Lourdes: "The water that flowed from the spring healed and purified. The fire of the candles shone out and rose to heaven, like a prayer. In the processions, we walked together toward the 'Promised Land.' In the grotto, pilgrims hid themselves in prayer." Everything spoke to these simple hearts. "And then," he added, "I noticed the transformation of the atmosphere at L'Arche upon our return – something lighter and warmer was in the air."[11]

In 1966, they made another pilgrimage, to Rome. This time, there were about a hundred people in seventeen vehicles. The following years, the little community left in three groups: one for Lourdes, another for La Salette, and a third for Fatima. They combined vacations with pilgrimages. From La Salette they traveled to Saintes-Maries-de-la-Mer; from Lourdes to Monserrat, in Spain; from Fatima in Portugal to Nazaré. They camped, swam, and had many adventures along the way. In 1968, their windshield exploded on the way to Spain, sparking off L'Arche member Dédé's enthusiasm. He danced around the car, saying, "It's so beautiful! It's so beautiful! It looks just like crystal!"[12]

UNLIKE L'ARCHE, FAITH AND LIGHT was international from the beginning. Its story began in the French countryside in 1967. Camille and Gérard Proffit, a farming couple who lived in the Somme, had two children with severe disabilities, Thaddée and Loïc. Neither was able to move or feed himself. Loïc was very small, too small for his eight years. He had trouble focusing his pale blue eyes on anything, and no one ever knew whether he could actually see what he was looking at or not. From time to time, he would strike his face violently or grunt, a sort of bitter laugh that distorted his features. Other times, he seemed to be smiling at shadows. Thaddée, his older brother, was bigger and heavier. He sat withdrawn in a wheelchair, coiled up as though he was trying to flee some danger only he could see. Like his brother, he only grunted.

Camille and Gérard wanted to join a pilgrimage to Lourdes that year and bring their children along with them. But the eager parents were told it was impossible to join the pilgrimage. The children would bother the other pilgrims and disturb the ceremonies. Besides, what was the use? They wouldn't understand anything anyway. Camille and Gérard decided to set out by themselves. They settled the two boys in their Citroën and traveled through France in the direction of Lourdes. Were they hoping for healing at the spring? Probably not. They were more likely looking for tenderness and reassurance. But they experienced a rude awakening upon their arrival: no hotel would take them in with their children. One suggested they leave the children at the Accueil Notre-Dame, a hospital. Finally, a hotel manager accepted them on the condition that the children eat in their room. The lonely family ate by themselves, and crept discreetly into the places of worship between the larger groups of pilgrims. The family encountered suspicious looks, pitying glances, and embarrassing remarks that hurt them. The intellectual disabilities of their sons instilled such fear!

Camille and Gérard shared the ordeal of those three days with Jean Vanier and Marie-Hélène Mathieu, a young woman who was president of the national teachers' union[13] and secretary general of OCH (Christian Office for Handicapped People), an organization that she had just founded along with a priest named Father

Bissonnier. In response, Jean and Marie-Hélène decided to set up pilgrimages for people with intellectual disabilities. With his ambition and her courage, they decided to "do it up big."

The little L'Arche group of thirty pilgrims that had lodged at the Cité Secours was nothing compared to the enormous international pilgrimage that inaugurated the Faith and Life movement. They would eventually recruit 17,000 pilgrims, and would require thirty chartered airplanes and eleven special trains to transport all of them to Lourdes! Such an undertaking inspired fear. And yet they began to plan, creating an association and forming teams. They focused on two essential components of a successful pilgrimage: spirituality and logistics.

Parents, educators, and priests agreed on the meaning and purpose of this pilgrimage, which some wanted to call a "gathering." In 1968, the word "pilgrimage" was considered to be old-fashioned in some circles, but the parents of those going were set on using it. In the end, it was Jean Vanier, with his knack for finding the middle ground, who proposed the term "International Pilgrimage-Gathering." Then, they agreed upon a name: Faith and Light. They wrote songs and put together a booklet that was translated into four languages. Meb, a painter with Down syndrome, designed the logo. They advertised the pilgrimage-gathering through every possible channel: in parishes, magazines, press releases, television, radio, and word of mouth.

In addition to tackling the financial, material, and medical questions of the pilgrimage, the planning team also had to fend off critics of the project. These critics warned that Jean and the other organizers were potentially endangering people with disabilities, who could react unpredictably when removed from their familiar routines. Further, they could feel even more humiliated if the daily demands of the pilgrimage reminded them of their deficiencies.

Others were unhappy with the choice of Lourdes, seeing it as not much more than a temple of religious knickknacks. In any case, how would they find enough hotel rooms for everyone? How far away was the nearest international airport? Some wondered if it was appropriate to invite Protestants or Anglicans into Lourdes, "Mary's town." Yet, the first L'Arche pilgrimage to Lourdes had included Anglican, Protestant, and Orthodox parents and friends of children with disabilities. As Marie-Hélène Mathieu writes in her passionate book telling this incredible story: "We were born ecumenical."[14]

Some clergy also raised questions about the pilgrimage, although Pierre-Marie Théas, the bishop of Tarbes and Lourdes, fervently supported the project – he even suggested pilgrimage dates over Easter. Others were more reticent, particularly in the Catholic Secretariat for Children and Youth with Disabilities (SCEJI),[15] despite the fact that Marie-Hélène Mathieu had a leadership role in the organization.

And then, there was the question of miracles. Would the pilgrimage raise false hopes that the spring at Lourdes would work miracles for pilgrims with intellectual disabilities, as it had for others with physical ailments? "We are not seeking physical healings," Jean Vanier replied. "The miracle we are looking for is to see the hearts of normal people open up and to watch as the barriers of rejection, contempt, fear, and exclusion fall away."[16]

Despite the opposition, criticism, and fears, the Faith and Light pilgrimage moved forward. The breadth of the project necessitated that they proceed step by step and take their time. And it took time – three years – not only because they had taken on so much, but because the very goal of the pilgrimage required it: to ensure that people with intellectual disabilities and their families no longer felt alone. They would not be arriving at Lourdes on their own, as the Proffit family had, but would be surrounded by friends. Before the pilgrimage, they formed communities of thirty or so people and got to know one another by gathering once or twice a month to pray, eat, and socialize. Within these groups, they formed smaller groups of three: a disabled child, a parent, and a friend. This allowed volunteers to form relationships with the disabled, and gave parents a helping hand. Jean and the Faith and Light team also arranged for doctors to take part in the pilgrimage and attend a colloquium on intellectual disabilities, scheduled for the same time. They could join the pilgrim groups, too, should the need arise. They would all arrive at Lourdes together, worship together, and celebrate together.

And there was indeed going to be a celebration! Jean Vanier recalls, "What we wanted was to provide a moment of great joy for these people who had been hurt for so long by contempt and rejection, hidden behind walls and constantly pushed aside, hurt because they were not trusted." On the great esplanade at Lourdes, which up until then had seen only processions and prayer meetings, a large podium with a sound system was set up. Christian musicians John Littleton and Raymond Fau were coming to sing. Each country, and each region, was invited to decorate a station and organize a performance, song, mime, or tableau vivant – a "living scene" featuring actors in a frozen pose. There would be parades in traditional costumes, a balloon release, a firework show, and dancing in front of the grotto.

There was one final, nagging criticism of the project: Wouldn't the pilgrimage aggravate the loneliness and sadness of those who had to return home after experiencing this fleeting, happy moment? Jean had the answer: "I think that once people have had a deep experience of joy, even if only once, something will open up in them. People who never believed they could be happy, who believed they did not have the right to be happy, if they have that experience even once, will be transformed in their inner being. Barriers in them will fall and something will blossom that had never been able to flourish, that had been stifled by too much fog and cold and hardness. . . . All people have to discover that they have the right to be happy."[17]

Easter 1971

DURING EASTER WEEKEND in 1971, the plan for the first Faith and Light meeting at Lourdes, three years in the making, was set in motion. Jean Vanier has said, "Each person must be taught that he or she has the right to be happy and that celebration and joy are possible on this earth." But the tentative pilgrims didn't seem to be aware of that yet. Four hundred and eighty people from Canada arrived on the first airplane, and they seemed rather intimidated, if not afraid. But there, at the foot of the walkway between the flight attendants and the pilots, stood the big, smiling Jean Vanier. He called out to them by name, shook their hands, and kissed them. Meanwhile, Marie-Hélène Mathieu was at the train station welcoming pilgrims, and later headed to the bus station to meet pilgrims who arrived by bus.

The April weather was cold and gray. In anticipation of the onslaught of pilgrims, the town seemed under siege. The police had set up roadblocks, the merchants had lowered their iron shutters, and barriers were set up along the rushing river with a soldier stationed every fifty yards to make sure no one got through and fell into the water. Frogmen – soldiers trained in scuba diving – were mobilized just in case!

Friday morning, each group of pilgrims headed for the grotto. As the communities' paths converged and crisscrossed, they saw many more people like themselves, and their confidence grew: "Here, parents feel no shame going out into the streets with their children. We are free here!" said one delighted woman. That afternoon, a welcome ceremony was held on the esplanade. Henri Donze, the new bishop of Tarbes and Lourdes, praised "the exceptional and prophetic character" of the pilgrimage, and Jean Vanier addressed twelve thousand pilgrims who had shown up the previous evening, as well as five thousand who had just arrived. He said, "Having come to Lourdes from every corner of France and the world, from fifteen countries, we believe that each one of us can become a bearer of hope. We have not come to weep, but to seek joy and to experience an encounter of peace. Together we must make the rivers of living water spring forth, for it is through them that we can grow a society of peace, love, and truth, where everyone is respected, loved, and can believe."[18] The emotion was intense, as though a balm had been poured over so many open and hidden wounds. Some were weeping tears of gratitude, and peace mingled with suffering and with the timid hope of joy.

In the following days the pilgrims participated in worship services, meetings, roundtable discussions, processions, and prayer vigils. The sky threatened rain, but day after day the shops opened their shutters, and pilgrims' faces shone. Joy was everywhere. The pilgrims with disabilities and their parents felt welcomed, respected, and loved at last. Their friends and assistants, as well as many people previously ignorant or indifferent to the lives of the disabled, were overwhelmed by such trust, simplicity, courage, and honesty. The closing celebration was an immense exultation that the rain, when it finally came, failed to extinguish. The rain blurred the colors of the fireworks, but it did nothing to dampen the laughing, singing, and dancing.

Jean Vanier never seemed to stop during those days at Lourdes. He was on site from early in the morning until late each evening to address, with Marie-Hélène Mathieu and the coordinating team, the inevitable problems that arose in bringing together such a big crowd. He gave press conferences, responded to requests from those who wanted to meet with him, met with officials, led roundtable discussions, and hosted the Easter Sunday prayer service, during which five thousand young people gathered together until late into the night. From the podium, he welcomed the crowds of pilgrims on the first day, launched the closing celebration, and sent everyone on their way with his blessing at the end. Jean was everywhere. But he was also discreet, almost invisible when – never in the front row – he prayed silently in the twilight of the immense underground basilica, while cries, grunts, murmurs, and sometimes a burst of laughter would echo from the vaulted ceiling during the singing.

ON MONDAY, THE DAY of departure, one Mass followed another, communities intermingled, and pilgrims kissed each other goodbye. The airplanes, trains, and buses were waiting. The pilgrimage had been an unequivocal success. Local hotel managers, authorities, and town residents had been conquered by the gentleness of the pilgrims. One chaplain wrote, "A wall fell, a wall not of refusal, but of ignorance." Even the press had been won over. Georges Hourdin wrote in *Le Monde:* "The wise of the world considered this world pilgrimage (things must be called by their real names) to be a foolish adventure. Why gather men and women who have wounded intelligence and, sometimes, motor dysfunction, at the risk of provoking serious accidents, discontent, and a sort of chaos? But it just so happens that reasonable people can be wrong.... During three days, from dawn until the heart of the night, the song of the pilgrimage rose into the skies of Lourdes in an immense, endlessly repeated hallelujah."[19]

The pilgrims set off for home, radiant. As they departed, Jean Vanier advised them, "Be faithful to the Holy Spirit. Continue to meet in communities of prayer, friendship, and mutual aid. Spark interest in celebrations and pilgrimages.... In several months we will get together again and take stock." The planners of the event gathered one last time. But was it really for the last time? No! They all wanted Faith and Light to continue. No one had really thought of continuing the program beyond this one pilgrimage. Marie-Hélène Mathieu would later write, "The Faith and Light pilgrimage was over, but the Faith and Light movement had just been born."[20]

The continuation of Faith and Light proved to be difficult, however. It was not the idea that posed a problem, nor a lack of enthusiasm, but questions of leadership and, perhaps, power. Could Faith and Light be an autonomous lay movement, or should it be managed by the Catholic hierarchy or connected to other organizations within the church? The debates were lively, and the attempts to promote self-interest were, too. Marie-Hélène Mathieu wrote convincingly, reminding everyone that Faith and Light had not been created by an organization and neither had it been the fruit of a hierarchical decision.

The communities for Faith and Light were already in place. These communities of friendship and prayer, the Faith and Light charter explained, must "work toward the integration of people with intellectual disabilities into the church and into society, to promote their physical and spiritual life and help them to grow in all their abilities."[21] Members did not live together, like at L'Arche, but they wove bonds of friendship, helped one another, and created spaces where people with disabilities and their parents needn't be ashamed of themselves. People listened to one another and celebrated together.

The memory of that first pilgrimage remained as well, and the pilgrims had departed full of fervor, determined to continue the gatherings. Existing communities were birthing new communities. Some L'Arche assistants returned to their home countries and founded new Faith and Light communities. Other people heard of Faith and Light through the Christian Office for Handicapped People, and joined the movement. Still other communities were inspired by Jean Vanier, who continued to introduce people to Faith and Light during his speeches and retreats around the world.

In 1971, one hundred and fifty Faith and Light groups came to Lourdes from fifteen countries. In 1981 there were three hundred groups in twenty-seven countries; in 1991, one thousand groups in sixty countries; in 2001, eleven hundred groups in seventy-three countries. Today there are one thousand, six hundred groups in eighty countries. Groups were founded in Poland, Slovenia, Brazil, and the Caribbean in the seventies; in Lebanon, Egypt, Syria, the

Philippines, and Zimbabwe in the eighties; in Ukraine, Argentina, and Rwanda in the nineties; and in Burkina Faso, Hong Kong, Iran, and Singapore in the early 2000s.

Passing the Torch

DURING THE SEVENTIES and eighties, L'Arche also continued to spread around the world. Jean Vanier followed the founding of each community closely. Developing the logistical and legal structures for Faith and Light had been relatively easy; for L'Arche it was harder but just as vital. So, along with other leaders, he participated in the formation of the board of directors for L'Arche, negotiated with authorities, sought out financing, and had discussions with professionals, institutions, and various religious authorities. He also met with people with disabilities and assistants and shared in the life of new homes, even if only for a few days. He also came back regularly to see the young communities.

Jean was the main reference point for the new founders, accompanying them on their journey. He writes:

> My role as guide is to listen to these assistants. I spend about
> an hour a month with each person, helping them to discern
> the causes of their personal and communal difficulties, and to
> understand their significance. It is a matter of meeting them
> where they are and not holding them up to an ideal standard or
> projecting what I think they should be. It's about helping them to
> find continuity between what they say and how they live, helping
> them to live in the reality of their humanity, and to understand
> and accept their gifts and capacities, but also their limits and
> wounds. Above all, it's about helping them to become human and
> grow in their spiritual life.[22]

Jean often gave responsibilities to young people who seemed little qualified – of course, in the early days of L'Arche, how could he do otherwise? – and to women who he felt had not yet taken their proper place in society. He had a tendency to trust people who had been overlooked by human resource departments, like Sue Mosteller. As a nun, she had lived most of her life in a convent. She did not speak French and she was afraid to travel by air. But Jean Vanier appointed her to be the first international coordinator of L'Arche. "It is a mark of L'Arche still today," says Stephan Posner, international leader of L'Arche, "that capacity to make risky nominations – for example, to appoint very young people to posts that demand a lot of responsibility."²³ Jean appointed Posner to be the director of a L'Arche community at only twenty-two. After he left L'Arche, he managed a small business, but felt compelled to return. Jean Vanier was not afraid to take risks, like putting his trust in Sue Mosteller and Stephan Posner. He maintained a faithful presence that confirmed, reassured, and helped things move forward. He communicated that trust – or put another way, faith – that was alive in him.

Jean could have tried to manage everything himself, but that was not what he wanted. He understood that besides the kind of leadership he had learned in the navy, where "the one in the know" is in command and makes all the decisions, there exists another kind of leadership: one that encourages growth. This kind of leadership accompanies, "listens, empowers, and provokes trust."²⁴ Barely a month after Philippe Seux arrived at the first L'Arche community, Jean Vanier had his first lesson in this kind of leadership. On the way to Mass with Philippe and Raphaël, whom he took with him every day, Raphaël asked him, "Why do I have to go to Mass?"

Why, in fact, did Jean take them along? He realized that he had not been taking their wishes into account enough. He wasn't considering their thoughts or the thoughts of the assistants, nor "leaving enough space to allow them to contradict if they so desired."²⁵ He realized that, first of all, he had to listen to them, that there was a difference between pointing out the way and imposing the path. The two forms of leadership can be combined, Jean admits. When there is a fire, he says, it is necessary to think and to decide quickly! But in community life, decisions have to be made together. As the current L'Arche leaders say: "At L'Arche, the decision-making process is as important as the results."

Eléna Lasida, a professor of economics at the Catholic Institute of Paris, writes that Jean Vanier was able to create "a power dynamic that is communal." The communal nature of L'Arche's organizational structure has the double merit of allowing everyone, even those with intellectual disabilities, to participate in the reflection and decision-making, while also helping everyone accept the responsibilities of others.

BY 1975, JEAN VANIER had already resigned from the post of international coordinator, and since 1980 he has held no official decision-making position in L'Arche. He wrote in 2011: "What was true thirty years ago does not apply today. Life is like a river: to hold back power is to impede the movement of life."[26] According to Eléna Lasida, "He knew how to let go and let others take the lead in their own way. This shift of the founder from the center toward the periphery is perhaps the strongest sign of the exercise of true collective and community power – a sign that I qualify as 'prophetic' for today's world. What we usually see is the opposite: power that ends up leading the one in power to believe that he or she is indispensable."[27] Unsurprisingly, Jean Vanier affirms that he didn't find it difficult to let go of the reins. "I let go," he says simply, "when I realized I was no longer able to keep up."[28]

Taking on the role of founder, director, and international coordinator from the beginning, however, had helped Jean get to the point of being able to relinquish a leadership role. These different roles required the capacity to understand problems and make rapid decisions, which sometimes made the job of the first board of directors seem a bit superfluous. During these creative years, Jean had proven to be indispensable. It was he who had set in place the coordinating bodies, overseen the discernment and reflection processes, and ensured that everything was functioning. This not only allowed L'Arche to end up with its unique type of governance, it also permitted Jean to step back at the right time, and enabled the continuance of a common spirit and true communion among L'Arche members despite the diversity in locations, languages, cultures, resources, and religions.

Viewed superficially, one might wonder what a large Canadian L'Arche house that was comfortable and richly blessed with subsidies had in common with the poverty of a L'Arche community in a slum in Tegucigalpa, or in a village in Burkina Faso. But it was not a matter of standardizing or defining a single mode of existence. Quite the opposite, it was a matter of allowing people to be themselves in a dynamic and fruitful relationship with others. That is, after all, the ultimate goal of L'Arche and Faith and Light: to knock down the barriers between individuals. To open oneself up to others in this way, without losing a sense of oneself, is only possible when one has a sense of belonging.

What is the L'Arche identity? What is the common element underlying all the communities? How is each community's own identity defined and preserved? In what ways are L'Arche communities different from other health care institutions? How is their Christian dimension different from a religious community? These are all questions that need to be revisited again and again at L'Arche and Faith and Light. One thing is certain: the unity among L'Arche members cannot emerge unless those who are the most fragile and weak have a place at the center of the community, and unless the joy of living together is of the utmost importance – regardless of the need for personal care and education.

JEAN VANIER'S RHYTHM of life in the seventies was truly staggering. In addition to overseeing new communities, giving retreats around the world, helping to coordinate the Faith and Light pilgrimage to Rome in 1975, and organizing the federations that regrouped L'Arche communities, he was also teaching in two schools for special education teachers and leading the

L'Arche community at Trosly. He still found time to keep up with his correspondence, publish books, and consult new Protestant, ecumenical, and interreligious communities.

Jean spent nearly all of his time moving from plane to train to bus. He received visitors until late into the night, visited care homes and psychiatric hospitals, spent time with people with disabilities and their parents, and met drug addicts and prisoners. He didn't spare himself at all, avoiding hotels wherever possible and traveling without comfort. All hunched up because of his size, he traveled third class in trains in India, in overcrowded buses on Latin American roads, and in economy class on airplanes – except four times a year, when Air Canada offered him flights in honor of his parents.

The pace of life soon became too much even for Jean Vanier, however. In 1976, he returned from a trip to India so sick that he had to be hospitalized. He stayed in the hospital for over two months. Thin, weakened, and bedridden, he was subject to erratic, severe fevers that worried the doctors. He slept poorly in a hospital bed that was too small for him, until a compassionate nurse remembered that they had a bed that had been custom made for General de Gaulle, who was also very tall. They retrieved it from a cellar where it had been carefully stored, awaiting the arrival of another giant. Nights were better in the general's bed. Eventually, the medicines did their job, and his liver and intestines began working well. The fever subsided. His appetite returned. He would have to relearn how to walk, but was finally released from the hospital and sent home to rest.

"During all that, Jesus taught me patience," he wrote in his letter to friends of April 27, 1976. In the hospital, Jean experienced weakness and discovered what it means to be the one who is helped rather than being the helper. He also learned to be detached, as he relinquished his leadership roles in L'Arche and Faith and Light to others. Jean wrote, "In reality, this was really a retreat, a time of prayer and offering; this was also a time of detachment: it was no longer the time to be the one in the leadership position, but the time to be weak and to abandon myself into the hands of God and to wait, believe, and trust."[29]

Twelve years had passed since the founding of L'Arche. What had once been a rather vague project was now a life's work – a work with a history, a clear message, and an identity that was confirming itself day by day.

7

Messenger

"HOW BEAUTIFUL ON THE MOUNTAINS are the feet of those who bring good news, who proclaim peace, who bring good tidings, who proclaim salvation, who say to Zion, 'Your God reigns'!"[1] How can we fail to apply these words from the prophet Isaiah to Jean Vanier? During the years following the founding at Trosly, he has been a tireless messenger of the Good News.

Even though Jean encouraged many others to found communities, even though he was driven by an urgency to provide dignified living conditions for people with intellectual disabilities, even though he recognized that these humiliated people deserved honor and sought to provide them with the place in society that they deserved, he never acted like he was trying to recruit others to "his" cause. He never intended to promote L'Arche or Faith and Light as though it were only his project. When he went to Rome to meet with the pope and other church hierarchy, or when he attended the annual meeting of bishops at Lourdes, he did not try to obtain recognition of his own work, nor to achieve any official status. He went to tell his church something. "He recognized the fact that he was the carrier of a message that had been entrusted to him," says Monsignor Gérard Daucourt, who met him while working in the Roman Curia. "He was not there to make L'Arche a success, but to bring this message."[2]

And he communicated this message with an astonishing freedom and forthrightness. Under the frescoes of the Vatican, for example, as he received the International Paul VI Award in 1997, he spoke tenderly to the ailing pope, John Paul II. It seemed that they were in for a long ceremony. The cardinal who had organized the event asked Jean Vanier to limit his speech to only a few minutes, and then on the day of the ceremony, he was asked to reduce it further. As the event proceeded, John Paul II listened – or at least seemed to listen – during the long speech by the bishop of Brescia, the hometown of Paul VI. After this, there was a long reply from the president of the prize committee. Finally, it was time for Jean Vanier to take the floor. "I was asked, Most Holy Father, to not talk too long, since you are tired," Jean said. The pope made a movement with his arm – was it exasperation or weariness? Jean continued, "It is fortunate that the disciples were not with Jesus, who was weary, when he sat down beside Jacob's Well. If they had been there, they would have prevented the approach of the Samaritan woman. And I think, Holy Father, that the Samaritan woman was a joy to Jesus. And we at L'Arche want to be a joy to you." John Paul II lifted his head. Looking at Jean Vanier, he rose and kissed him.

Jean Vanier has candidly delivered the same message in many places. A mufti invited him to speak to an assembly of seven hundred Muslims in Damascus; he addressed eight hundred Anglican bishops at the ten-year meeting of the Anglican Communion in Lambeth Palace; and he spoke to fifteen hundred listeners at the great hall of UNESCO in Paris. He met with a tiny American Indian tribe in the north of Canada, and with groups of high school students and teachers in the United States.

His message is not meant for one specific audience – Catholics or Protestants, Muslims or Hindus, believers or atheists, people with disabilities or healthy people, those who are marginalized or those who are not, the rich or the poor. No, his message is for everyone. When Jean speaks, it is usually about L'Arche and people with intellectual disabilities, and the need to provide justice for this small, humiliated group that suffers rejection in virtually every culture. But his message extends far beyond L'Arche and questions of disability. More profoundly, he questions our society as a whole, and each person in it – our ways of living and our fundamental choices. What he says about our personal responsibility toward ourselves and others is quite unsettling. That may be why his listeners often try to limit the scope of his speeches to the intellectually disabled and those who care for them. One of the typical responses that most saddens Jean Vanier is, "What a magnificent work you have accomplished, and how good it is to care for these poor people in such a way!"

Jean Vanier does not "take care of" people with intellectual disabilities. He lives with them. He lives with L'Arche members Eric, Doudou, Pauline, and René. Jean Vanier does not give talks about people with intellectual disabilities. He speaks about what it means to be human, about humanity and society as a whole. But how did he come to this understanding of humanity?

As a former professor and a specialist in Aristotle, Jean reflected on the Aristotelian definition of man as a rational animal. He also searched for answers among other philosophers, such as Emmanuel Lévinas and Martin Buber, who refer to humans as relational beings.

As a former theology student, he looked to the "Angelic Doctor" Thomas Aquinas, as well as to the mystics. He especially looked to the Bible, which he never ceased to study, scrutinize, and probe in order to uncover its "pith and marrow." He also consulted Indian thinkers, particularly Mahatma Gandhi. He was continually seeking, hoping to find that "still, small voice" that allows us to be ourselves and to attain the fullness of our being.

Jean also sought answers in psychiatry. He met with the psychiatrist Dr. Thompson at Eau Vive, and after becoming director of Val Fleuri, he spent time with Léone Richet, Erol Franko, Patrick Mathias, and the various L'Arche psychiatrists in Trosly. He watched them at work, read their writings, attended their lectures, and absorbed their theories and their experiences.

As a former naval officer, he looked for answers in his training, his experience as cadet captain at Dartmouth Royal Naval College, and the discipline he learned on the *Frobisher* and *Vanguard*.

But it was daily life at L'Arche – giving baths, preparing meals, handling the violence and anguish of these social outcasts but also their freedom and tenderness – that taught him about our deepest longing.

Jean Vanier's thought has been watered by these various springs. To truly appreciate his message, one must have a sense not only of the theoretical, but also of the practical. Jean loves to say that his vision "emerged progressively, and only progressively, from pragmatism."[3] His thought – like the humanity he speaks about – is a strange harmony between matter and spirit that we find so hard to bring to expression in ourselves, we who are both the ground where experience takes place and the ones who receive the breath of the Spirit.

Jean Vanier's message, like the message of the gospel, is not primarily an abstract explanation of the world, but is rather an encounter with a person, the affirmation of a hope, and an invitation to follow a path to places we will only discover if we dare to take it.

The Message Is the Messenger

WHAT DRAWS SO MANY different people from diverse cultures – the young, especially – to Jean Vanier's message is his authentic way of speaking. When he speaks, he never takes on a false persona; he never tries to impose his thoughts or manipulate anyone. He connects to others by being totally himself and totally open – it is obvious where he's coming from and what his reference points are. He is Christian and Catholic, which he affirms clearly, yet everyone is able to receive his message, because he is neither militant nor dogmatic. He respects the freedom of his listeners. His delivery is forceful but not adversarial. The witness of his life and the choices he has made give him credibility, too.

In 1985, Stephan Posner, who would become the international leader of L'Arche, was twenty-one years old. He was Jewish, but not so sure that he was really a believer. Did God exist? A rabbi told him that was a question for Christians! Posner wasn't interested in disabilities or Catholicism. He was a conscientious objector to military service in search of a place to do his required alternative service, and he hoped to find an activity in the area of alternative economics. Someone suggested L'Arche to him, and he accepted without knowing much about it. One evening, the members of his community decided to go hear Jean Vanier, who was giving a speech, and he went with them.

> I don't remember very clearly what he said, but I know that he spoke to me. He spoke to me, even though he came from a completely different world with reference points that were very different from mine. His talk was punctuated by references to Jesus and God. At that time, the very word "spirituality" was suspect to me. But there was something in what he said, perhaps especially in the way in which it was said without empty words, something that pushed beyond cultural barriers and representations and preconceptions my preconceptions. And that, I believe, is a trademark of Jean Vanier. When you listen to him, it rings true. There is something very distinctive in his way of speaking. He is what he says. With him, the message is the messenger. This man impressed me very much; what he was saying reached me. He told a story, a story that brought together what we humans have in common. A universal story. My story.[4]

This encounter with Jean Vanier inspired Stephan Posner to commit his life to the L'Arche movement.

Jean's word rang true for Posner and others because there is complete continuity between who he is and what he expresses. "He is a man of absolute simplicity and sincerity," says Gérard Daucourt. Words play a small part in conveying a message compared to everything else – look, attitude, gestures, tone of voice – that communicates to those who are listening. People with disabilities who don't understand the words very well are particularly sensitive to that "music of being," to use Jean Vanier's expression, but we all hear it. We all perceive if a speaker's manner of delivery is in harmony with the words he or she speaks. With Jean, that music of being accords so precisely with what he is saying that, says French-Canadian philosopher Jacques Dufresne, "from a messenger like Jean Vanier, I would be tempted to believe everything he says, so much am I sensitive to all that he is."[5]

Jean's message is also rooted in stories: his story, the stories of the people he lives with, and the stories of the thousands of people he has met. Because of this, his message never feels disembodied. He grasps – first of all in himself, then in others – the enthusiasm, joy, rejection, fear, anxiety, and certainty that mingle in the human heart, that heart which, the Bible tells us, is deceitful, desperately sick, and inscrutable.[6] Jean often talks about himself and the path he has taken: of the trust his father showed him, the beginnings of L'Arche, and the evolution of his thought. But he doesn't give the impression that he's only talking about himself. He is not only a guide and master; he is a brother and a fellow traveler. He never places himself on a pedestal; what he says about himself tells us about ourselves.

Jean speaks from experience and from the knowledge he has drawn from that experience. The verb "to do" is an important one for Jean Vanier. He distrusts ideologies. He only relies on theories to the extent that they shed light on everyday life. For him, "reality is the master."[7]

And so, when a journalist, surprised to see him doing the dishes after a meal at Val Fleuri, asked him, "Why are you doing the dishes?" his answer was, "Because they're dirty!" This quip also points to a simple truth: we have to do what needs to be done. The act of performing a task is its own end. This is part of his message: do useful tasks because they need to be done and not for a selfish reason or for some future reward. It's a message of humility and simplicity. The Good Samaritan who approached the wounded man, unlike the Levite who turned away, was not thinking first about himself or the consequences of his actions. He was moved at the sight of the man and was thinking about what needed to be done: he staunched the flow of blood, dressed the wounds, poured wine and oil, and took him to a place he could be cared for and recover. Jean, like the Samaritan, tends to the immediate needs around him.

"We Will Do and We Will Understand"

"WE WILL DO and we will understand,"[8] the Hebrew people answered Moses, when he presented them with the tablets of the Law and proclaimed the covenant with God. This response might seem strange to us; we would tend to invert the terms, not committing ourselves to obeying the commandments before we fully understand them. Yet this ordering – trusting, obeying, and acting first – is fundamental to the life of faith; Christian philosopher Blaise Pascal calls it the "order of charity." Jean Vanier lives according to this order. He is a man of faith, a man who trusts the injunctions of the Bible that we too often see as beautiful, but impossible, words.

One day, while Jean was walking along a street with friends in Trosly, he was confronted by a man who was raving mad. The man had just come from a home where he had been making a disturbance. He approached Jean, gesticulated, and threatened. He shouted, "I'm going to hit you! You people at L'Arche, you have bathrooms, you have everything. I don't have anything. I'm going to hit you!" Jean stood motionless between the man and the little terrified group that accompanied him. "Hit me, if you want to," he said. The man struck him in the face with such violence that Jean would remain deaf in one ear for the rest of his life. He who was so big let himself be struck and did not answer blow for blow. Instead he said, "You can hit me again if you want to."

In that moment, perhaps Jean remembered Christ's words in the Gospel of Matthew, "You have heard that it was said: 'Eye for eye, and tooth for tooth.' But I tell you, do not resist an evil person. If anyone slaps you on the right cheek, turn to him the other cheek also."⁹ Or perhaps he had absorbed the words of Christ so deeply that they had become part of him, guiding his reaction without him even thinking about it. Was he overcome with pity in the face of the blind violence of that man? Was he afraid? Yes, Jean says. He was very scared, but he did what seemed right. He didn't run away. He didn't retaliate. The man calmed down immediately, took his hand, and said, "Let's drink some lemonade together at my home." Jean followed him home. In the courtyard a German shepherd growled and stirred. "He won't hurt you," said its master. The two men shared a drink in the kitchen.

In the same spirit of the gospel, while settling into the first L'Arche community with Philippe and Raphaël, Jean followed to the letter Jesus' injunction in Luke: "When you give a luncheon or dinner, do not invite your friends, your brothers or sisters, your relatives, or your rich neighbors. . . . But when you give a banquet, invite the poor, the crippled, the lame, the blind . . ." Jean Vanier's table included the crippled, the lame, and the blind. And each time he accepted an award, it was only on the condition that his L'Arche companions, who broke bread with him every day, would be invited to accompany him to receive it.

"We will do and we will understand," says the Bible. Pascal says something similar: "We say that it is necessary to know human beings before we can love them. . . . The saints, on the contrary, say in speaking of divine things that it is necessary to love them in order to know them, and that we only enter truth through charity."¹⁰ There are existential truths that we must commit to in order to know them, at the risk of being transformed by them. We cannot contemplate them from outside, as we might observe some object. There are truths that have to become part of us if we want to comprehend them.

These truths that must be loved, practiced, and engaged with if we want to understand them are what Christianity calls "mystery." Jean Vanier speaks to us about this mystery, which he is careful to distinguish from a secret. In his book *Signs of the Times* he writes, "While a secret can be revealed, leaving nothing more to say about it, a mystery is never exhausted. One can always plunge further into it. I really mean 'plunge,' because a mystery is a dwelling place: we don't contain it; it is greater than we are and it contains us. A secret lives in us, but we live in a mystery."[11]

It was in this spirit that Jean addressed priests in Rome in 2012:

> I would like to be a messenger to you, transmitting this mystery that can't be explained, that we at Faith and Light and L'Arche are called to experience and to announce. Saint John began his letter to the Christian communities by evoking his life experience: "That which was from the beginning, which we have heard, which we have seen with our eyes, which we have looked at and our hands have touched – this we proclaim concerning the Word of life."[12] I can only tell you about what we have experienced.

What Jean has experienced is poignant. Unexpected. But unheard of? No, for we read in the Gospels: "I praise you, Father, Lord of heaven and earth, because you have hidden these things from the wise and learned, and revealed them to little children."[13] And Paul, in the First Letter to the Corinthians, is just as clear: "But God chose the foolish things of the world to shame the wise; God chose the weak things of the world to shame the strong. God chose the lowly things of this world and the despised things . . . so that no one might boast in the presence of God."[14]

GOD HAS REVEALED his mysteries to little children; he has chosen the weak of the world to shame the strong. But this is difficult to hear and believe. Jean Vanier didn't believe it in the beginning, either. The man who settled in Trosly with Philippe and Raphaël in 1964 thought he knew what he was doing. At least, he knew what he wanted: shocked by the living conditions of people with intellectual disabilities, he wanted to give them a more dignified life and to help them be fulfilled. He had few doubts that he would know what must be done and how they should live. He was wise and well-educated. He was cultured, efficient, organized, generous, and religious. But he quickly discovered that these were not qualities that mattered for his new companions. Little did he know at that time that they were the ones who would help him understand himself. It was they, the weak and despised ones, who would become his "masters in humanity," in a way that was totally upside-down for him.[15]

> I discovered that we grew together and that it was they who helped to fulfill me, they who little by little revealed to me my humanity, they who led me further and further into a world of friendship and communion that healed my heart and awakened life in me. Yes, I knew how to do things, I knew how to organize, lead, and teach. I could be efficient, but I discovered that that was not primarily what they wanted from me. They wanted what was most important: a presence, a relationship, love.[16]

What Philippe and Raphaël wanted was a friend, someone who could simply be happy in their company, someone who would love them just as they were. "Living with Philippe and Raphaël, these two men who were so fragile and weak, having suffered so much from rejection, I discovered that everyone thirsts for communion with other human beings."[17] What surprised Jean was that he found that same thirst in himself. He discovered that there is a wounded child hiding in each of us, a child who has been calling in vain, whom we wall up and silence with our social standards, professional titles, and personal successes. We have hidden this inner child behind so many walls that we have eventually forgotten him.

Yet he is awakened in us by the cry of the poor, by their raw thirst for relationships and love, their inability to play the social games of power and prestige, their inability to disguise their feelings, and their lack of satisfaction with those superficial relationships that we settle for all too often.

Life shared with Philippe and Raphaël shook the defenses that Jean Vanier had built up around his inner child – those barriers that had protected the young Jean who was alienated from his depressive mother, who witnessed the suffering of his amputee father, who remembered the cries of the refugees abandoned by the *Nariva*, who left his family at thirteen without a tear, and who was carried away by waves that nearly drowned him. Jean Vanier rediscovered in himself that vulnerable, loving child that was made for happiness and joy, the child the Gospels say we must become if we want to enter the kingdom.

Cardinal Rylko, president of the Pontifical Council for the Laity, has called L'Arche a revolution: "You people at L'Arche and at Faith and Light," he declared one day, "have created a veritable Copernican revolution. It is no longer you doing good to disabled people. You tell yourself that it is they who are doing you good!" Like Jean Vanier in 1964, volunteers still arrive at L'Arche driven by generosity or concerned about justice. They come to help the poor, hardly imagining that the poor might be able to help them. But then, Jean says, the encounter with these people who are weak and suffering "transforms, little by little, their generosity into true love, compassion, and tenderness."[18] They discover that they, too, are vulnerable and fragile, but at the same time capable of loving and being strengthened by the power of love.

Eric

IN 1980, JEAN VANIER decided to resign from his position as director of the Trosly community and take a year's sabbatical. The following year, in November, he moved to La Forestière, a L'Arche community for people with severe disabilities that had opened in 1978. This had been a dream of his for a long time.

La Forestière, surrounded by the forest, as its name suggests, was a new, one-story building constructed around a bright central patio. It was flooded with light from the large bay windows that opened onto the garden. There was a fireplace in the large room where one could stop for a cup of coffee or for evening prayers. It had a small chapel with a very low altar that allowed a person with disabilities, stretched out on the knees of an assistant seated on the ground, to see what was happening. The atmosphere was peaceful. People here took their time; the community seemed to move in slow motion. This was a place where there was plenty of time to get close to one another, so that someone who is blind and deaf could touch a person who approaches. There was plenty of time to bathe Eric – a resident whose body was curled up by disability and despair – slowly unknotting his limbs, letting him feel the warm water, letting him play with the soap, washing him. There was plenty of time to feed Lucien, so that he might feel the pleasure of tasting, swallowing, and smelling the food. These broken bodies[19] were touched with respect and tenderness. While someone gently wiped away the saliva dripping down Henriette's chin, someone else gently took hold of the hand of Loïc, who had just struck himself violently on the nose. They restrained him without harshness, respecting what he might have been trying to express by his actions, reassuring him that he had been heard, and he was not alone.

At La Forestière one must learn to understand the language of the body. It is a language of tenderness and frailty. The body, which is exalted in athletics and fashion and despised in sickness, aging, and disability – this same body is, the apostle Paul writes, a temple of the Holy Spirit.[20] The broken body, then, is a broken temple that lets the light of God pass through more easily. Jean Vanier knows that the Gospel is the story of a God who chose to be born in human form, with all its brokenness and frailty:

The Word did not become flesh
in the same way one puts on a piece of clothing
only to discard it again;
it is flesh becoming divine,
becoming the means by which that life of love
from God
in God
communicates itself.
That life is not an idea that can be learned
from books or teachers;
it is the presence of one person to another,
the total giving of oneself to another,
heart to heart,
in a communion
of love.[21]

As Francis of Assisi's encounter with lepers allowed him to discover "a new softness in his body and spirit," La Forestière was a decisive new step in the life of Jean Vanier. For a year, he experienced the rhythm of life with these men and women with severe disabilities – the rhythm of Eric, for instance, a seventeen-year-old who was blind, deaf, and unable to walk or feed himself. Abandoned in a hospital at four years of age, he was so desperate for human contact that he clung with all the strength in his arms to anyone who passed close to him. Jean discovered that Eric reciprocated all the love he showed him. Jean washed, clothed, fed, and calmed him, reassuring him by these actions that he could be loved, and therefore that he was lovable. For his part, Eric introduced Jean to a new form of peace. Jean writes:

> At La Forestière, every evening after dinner, I put Eric in his
> pajamas, then we spent a half or three-quarters of an hour in
> prayer, all of us together in the living room, both the disabled
> people and the assistants. I often sat with Eric on my knees; he
> rested. And I discovered that I rested with him. I didn't feel like

talking. I was at peace, with an inner quiet. He also was at peace; he also felt content. It was a moment of healing. I found inner harmony again.[22]

But those times when Eric clammed up, howling and writhing, when nothing could calm him down and he was overwhelmed by darkness, Jean Vanier found a door opened to hidden distress, violence, and fear buried in his own heart. He discovered a whole world of chaos and hate within himself that he had carefully masked with his education and intelligence or buried in his work and activities.

Reflecting on such angst is a recurring theme in Jean's thought. He has realized that it is an inescapable part of the human condition. "Cows do not experience anguish," he jokes. Contained in a secret part of our being, this anguish can emerge suddenly, along with the violence it produces, at the least hurt. Jean says he still feels within himself today that "it is like a bomb ready to explode, driving us to call for help."[23]

Discovering his own inner violence has allowed him to recognize similarities between himself and the intellectually disabled he cares for, similarities to which he had previously been blind. He feels as though he has been knocked off an invisible pedestal – his goodness – which is humiliating, but also liberating. "I have been brought face to face with my own deep reality, with my own truth. . . . I begin to be myself. I no longer play the great and powerful grownup, striving for first place, for success, and for admiration; I am no longer worried about appearances. I allow myself to be the child that I am, the child of God."[24]

At La Forestière, then, it is no longer a question of Jean Vanier and Eric – the adult and the miserable child – but of "two children playing a game of the soul," a game which, the poet Pierre Emmanuel tells us, connects us to "the fields of eternity" where all springs of love find their superabundant source.[25] Communion – that other word for love – allows us to be together in God, Love Himself, who unites and gathers us. Eric evokes this mystery of peace and union in anyone who comes close to him and takes time with him, because he does not ask for anything more, and does not try to control or dominate or use anyone.

In his relationship with Eric, Jean Vanier was finally able to understand this sentence from the Gospels that he had heard many times: "Whoever welcomes this little child in my name welcomes me; and whoever welcomes me welcomes the one who sent me. For it is the one who is least among you all who is the greatest."[26] Jean reflected in a newsletter, "This is the mystery that is revealed to us in L'Arche today: the poorest person leads us directly to the heart of God. The smallest one heals our wounds, sometimes by painfully revealing them to us. And that healing and that experience of Jesus and his Father come through the heart-to-heart relationship of mutual trust that grows between us."[27]

The Taste of Happiness

BY PUTTING INTO PRACTICE these beautiful and often seemingly impossible words of Scripture, Jean Vanier has also found that they accomplish what they promise. He is sensitive to what he calls the hidden Beatitudes – those promises of happiness and blessing that run through the Gospels. There are many of these promises: "Blessed rather are those who hear the word of God and obey it."[28] "Blessed is the one who will eat at the feast in the kingdom of God."[29] "Blessed are those servants whom the master finds awake when he comes."[30] "Blessed are those who have not seen and yet have believed."[31] And Jesus concludes, after washing his disciples' feet: "Now that you know these things, you will be blessed if you do them."[32]

The founder of L'Arche has a taste for beatitude – for happiness. Delight, joy, gladness, and happiness are key terms in his vocabulary and account greatly for the choices he has made in life. The happy community in the Harlem Friendship House prodded him to leave the navy. His dissertation dealt with Aristotle's happiness. And it was the delight of living in L'Arche that kept him there. He wrote to his friend Julia Kristeva, "What is the secret that enables L'Arche to still exist? I'm going to tell you: *it is delight.* If people come to live in L'Arche and stay for a month, a year, or forty years, it's because they are happy and experience delight. No assistant would stay here out of duty or because they had to. No one would stay just to do a good deed."[33] The delight Jean speaks of springs from true, stable relationships and from the fight against darkness; a delight that opens a path through tears and suffering; a delight that, as Aristotle said, is born out of every free action. But it is also delight in the freedom to finally be oneself, freedom from the tyranny of normalcy, which crushes us with all its demands.

AS A BOY, Jean didn't like formal balls and receptions. As a sailor, he preferred chapels to night clubs at ports of call. Nevertheless, he loves parties and celebrations. "Celebration," he writes in *Community and Growth,* "is a cry of joy and thankfulness because our lives have been woven together, because we are connected one to another, because we belong to the same body, because our differences represent a treasure and richness, because we can let fall the barriers that separate us from one another. We rejoice when we can unveil that which is deepest and most vulnerable: the fact that we are linked together by trust."[34]

Jean Vanier's message is primarily an invitation to joy: "There are so many people who are unaware that celebration and joy are possible on this earth," he said at Lourdes in 1971. Many L'Arche volunteers report experiencing the "perfect joy" that Jesus promises in the Gospels: "These things I have spoken to you, that my joy may be in you, and that your joy may be full."[35] Joy abounds in the relationships among L'Arche community members. The intellectually disabled, whose disabilities sometimes prevent them from possessing what seems basic to human happiness, are nonetheless bearers of joy. And there is joy to be found in living with them.

HAVING SAID THAT, Jean Vanier is well aware that life can be difficult when shared with suffering people who, at times, confront us with our own weaknesses. We fear forming relationships with disabled people because they carry a patently visible mark of death. Very much in spite of themselves, they have trespassed on a boundary that it is forbidden to cross. This atrophied arm, that twisted mouth, this disoriented mind, they seize us with horror – that same horror that can also sometimes take hold of us in the presence of the sacred. People with disabilities mix up life and death in themselves in an unbearable way. This is true, in lesser measure, of all who have failed, who aren't able to cope in the world as it is: the sick, the vulnerable, the unemployed, the homeless, and the poor. In our fear of what their imperfections represent, we find that the easiest thing to do is to exclude them.

But what the Gospels say – which Jean Vanier repeats and which people experience at L'Arche – is that by forming relationships with those who are poor, wounded, excluded, and humiliated, no longer avoiding them and thereby avoiding our own wounds but admitting our inherent vulnerability, we will embark on a journey of hope and happiness.

This mystery, though incomprehensible, is a promise, as the prophet Hosea writes, "I will . . . make the Valley of Achor a door of hope."[36] Jean Vanier notes that the Valley of Achor lies near Jericho, a place of misfortune, of cursed gorges where demons and ferocious beasts prowl, a place travelers avoid at all costs. This is the valley God asks us to pass through so that we may find the door to hope. This experience of "passing through," for the Christian, is expressed in terms of the cross and the resurrection. Those who come into contact with L'Arche, whether believers or unbelievers, can sense this mystery at work in the movement. In the words of a young volunteer, "something on the side of death becomes fulfillment and life."

One must experience how fruitful vulnerability and weakness can be before one can hope to fully understand them. Jean Vanier remembers having breakfast with Pope John Paul II in 1987. At that time, the media was still describing the pope as "God's athlete." Jean spoke to him about Eric – how Eric was transforming Jean's heart because of his severe disabilities. The pope listened, but as he left the room, he remarked, "I have no idea what he was talking about!" In 1996, however, news broke that John Paul II had been diagnosed with Parkinson's disease. The pope entered little by little into the mystery Jean had spoken about. In a 2004 message, John Paul II described people with intellectual disabilities as "humanity's privileged witnesses," and as "living icons of the cruci-fied Son" and "heralds of a new world that is no longer dominated by force and violence and aggressiveness, but by love, solidarity, and acceptance."[37]

In August of 2004, John Paul II asked the founder of L'Arche to lead a meditation during the pope's visit to Lourdes. Jean walked several steps ahead of the popemobile. The pope's Parkinson's had continued to worsen. He was slumped in his armchair and found it difficult to speak. Jean said to the crowd, "Our Holy Father is frail and doing poorly, but he is the glory of God. God mani-fests himself through him." After speaking, Jean Vanier thought he would slip away discreetly. But John Paul II called him back, caressed his cheek, and gave him his rosary beads. "He knew that I loved him in his weakness, just as I knew he loved L'Arche and me in our weakness,"[38] Jean wrote.

The Path toward Freedom

THE DOOR TO HOPE is also the door to deliverance from fear. We no longer need to be afraid of other people, nor of ourselves. We can set aside the masks we typically wear. We can form true relationships in which people are not our adversaries, but brothers and sisters who gently reveal our frailty and affirm our beauty as human beings. As Jean Vanier says: "You are much more beautiful than you dare to believe."

The first step on the path to this kind of freedom is to let go of the many fears that paralyze and imprison us: the fear of not being loved, the fear of failure, of being different, of judgment, of exclusion, of change, of losing one's possessions. These fears shape us in accordance with the expectations of our parents, teachers, friends, or society, and we lose our true selves along the way. Jean Vanier calls us to the freedom that allows us to grow into who we truly are. To be free, he writes in *Becoming Human*, is to die to the "false me"[39] of our social constructs and fears, and to welcome in our real self, this unique "I" that is indispensable to others and to the world.

Jean Vanier is the kind of spiritual teacher who leads people to freedom, even if it means, ultimately, letting them go. How many people have found their way at L'Arche and then left for a monastery, a seminary, or some other path! Yet Jean doesn't feel they owe him anything, for he does not think he owns anyone or anything – not even the L'Arche movement that he founded. "It is often said that I am the founder," he said recently at an anniversary celebration of L'Arche communities, "but I am simply the first one who arrived." Those who took over the management of L'Arche after him have been completely free to create their own paths. We all feel like founders, they say. We are the children of L'Arche, for that is what he handed over to us: freedom.

WHEN WE ARE FREE, we are also collectively responsible for the living conditions we impose on others, especially those who are most fragile and who cannot grow and blossom if we do not provide fertile ground. In most societies, those with intellectual disabilities are subjected to a dreadful double penalty: their disability also results in their exclusion from society. What inhuman judge, what invisible tribunal, has been allowed to pronounce such a heavy sentence? "You were born without arms, a virus has destroyed your intelligence, a gene mutation or one too many chromosomes will prevent you from learning how to read and write or taste and know the beauty of the world. And so," the cruel judge's sentence continues, "you are also condemned to be excluded from human society. You will live chained to a tree or shut up in an asylum. And if your parents do not abandon you, they will be very alone in caring for you." Yet in dealing out this sentence, society cripples itself by depriving itself of the qualities that people with disabilities draw out of others: gentleness, perhaps, and another vision of the world. This vision of the world sometimes seems absurd in the eyes of the strong.

Nadine Tokar, a L'Arche founder who also helped organize the first Special Olympics in 1970, remembers one race in particular. Early on, a young man broke away from the pack and ran ahead. He wasn't far from crossing the finish line when he turned around and saw the others behind him. He retraced his steps and took their hands, and the runners crossed the finish line together. What a different understanding of the world – an understanding that has much to teach us!

In any case, this is what Jean Vanier thinks. He reminds us that in our competitive society, "some people win, many people lose, and an even greater number of people are victims."[40] Therefore, he says, we have to dare to be free. We have to escape the diktat of competition and rivalry, not because they are bad in them-selves – they can arouse in us positive energies that encourage us to surpass ourselves – but because seen as absolutes and the only way of operating, they create a society that becomes more and more inhuman. We have to approach things differently; we have to leave the beaten path, sometimes without knowing where we are going.

Jean Vanier decided to join the military at the age of thirteen, at a time when one ship out of five sank in the Atlantic. He settled with Philippe and Raphaël in Trosly in the most precarious of conditions. He launched a L'Arche community in India and one in the Palestinian territories. He recognized that in the eyes of reason, these initiatives were absurd. Yet he listened to that inner voice, his conscience, that was deeper than habits or acquired certainties. Speaking at UNESCO in January 2014, he said that conscience is not primarily "the ability to discern good from bad, but an attraction toward freedom and justice, toward the good and the beautiful. This is the same attraction that is active in nature, drawing everything toward light, harmony, and love."[41]

And when we follow that attraction toward freedom, he added, it feels like we have come home, like we have reconnected with the deep truths of our inner selves. This is a place of peace, an inner sanctuary where, in silence, God waits for us to find him, "because that deepest of attractions directs us to God, who wants us to be fulfilled men and women." Jean Vanier often quotes Etty Hillesum, who writes, "There is in me a very deep well, and at the bottom of this well, there is God. Sometimes I manage to reach him, but most of the time stones and rubble obstruct this well, and so God is buried. I must bring him into the light."

Choosing freedom often brings inner struggle. When that attraction to L'Arche arose in Odile Ceyrac's heart at the dinner table with Raphaël and the others in Trosly, she fought it at first. She went back to her day-to-day life. But then, one evening, she told a certain friend about Raphaël's gaze, and about her instinct that her place was there, with L'Arche. She expected her friend to laugh, but he didn't; he looked at her and said, "That's serious." Odile wept about it the whole night. By morning she had made up her mind, and with that, a great peace and joy filled her: "I had found my homeland."[42]

The Message of Peace

As Jesus drew near to Jerusalem, he wept. . . .
Jesus wept: "If you had only understood the message of peace . . ."
. . . Jesus weeps over our world today.
He weeps over our countries where inequality, division, and exclusion are so dominant.

THUS BEGINS *Befriending the Stranger* by Jean Vanier. Jean has followed this example of Jesus, weeping over the divisions in our world. He is accustomed to saying that the work of God is unity. "The most intimate thought of Jesus," he repeats often, "is to gather together all the dispersed children of God. That is why he came. What makes a person human is the work he or she undertakes on behalf of peace and unity."[43]

For Jean, peace begins with encounters, like that meeting between Francis of Assisi and the sultan in 1219, during full-scale war between Christians and Muslims. Did Francis want to convert the sultan, or instruct him in the Christian faith? No one knows. But Saint Bonaventure, who related the story, describes a joyful encounter: "The sultan listened to him with pleasure and pressed him to stay longer with him." And Albert Jacquard writes, "It seems that the sultan never forgot Francis's smile and gentleness. . . . Perhaps this memory had a decisive effect, because ten years later, although no force compelled him, he returned Jerusalem to the Christians."[44]

Jean, who has called himself a child of war, is a messenger of peace. He is dedicated to bringing down barriers and walls, whether symbolic or real: the Berlin Wall that cast its shadow on the world for so long; the wall that separates Israel from the Palestinian territories; and all the walls we raise between groups and within ourselves. He writes, "The greatest affliction of the human being is separation and isolation. It always produces guilt, anger, vengeance, jealousy, and other things of the same type. These all lead to war and are a foretaste of death."[45]

As soon as he was able, Jean traveled to the other side of the Iron Curtain, breaking symbolic barriers even as physical barriers remained. He helped to create a clandestine L'Arche community in Poland in 1981, and in 1985, Faith and Light invited him to hold retreats there. In Bucharest in 1992, he gathered together Catholics, Protestants, and Orthodox at the Orthodox Institute of Theology. In 1993, he preached in Slovenia and Bosnia. And when he was asked to hold his first retreat in the Ukraine in 1993, he accepted on the condition that three branches of the Orthodox church – the Greek Orthodox Church, the Orthodox Church under the Patriarch of Kiev, and the Russian Orthodox Church under the Patriarch of Moscow – join the Pentecostals and Baptists.

Jean then laid down a second condition: a foot-washing ceremony. He required this at a 1995 retreat in Northern Ireland that gathered together Catholic bishops, bishops of the Church of Ireland, Presbyterian pastors, Methodists, and representatives of the Salvation Army. He required the same humble ceremony in 1997 at the Ecumenical Council of Churches in Geneva, where representatives of 145 churches gathered, as well as in 1998 at a global gathering of Anglican bishops at Lambeth Palace.

"Don't Hide from Your Own Flesh and Blood."

THE SCENE in the Gospel of John where Christ washes the feet of the disciples is a familiar one. During the Last Supper on Holy Thursday, Christ stood up, took off his outer garment, and girded himself with a towel. He took up a basin of water and set about washing the feet of the disciples. Jesus told them, "You do not realize now what I am doing, but later you will understand." For most of us, it remains only a scene.

Jean Vanier, though, has noticed that once Jesus had washed the feet of everyone, including those of his betrayer, he said, "Do you understand what I have done for you? You call me 'Teacher' and 'Lord,' and rightly so, for that is what I am. Now that I, your Lord and Teacher, have washed your feet, you also should wash one another's feet. I have set you an example that you should do as I have done for you."[46]

Christ is asking us to help one another and not hesitate to take on the humblest task. In ancient times foot washing was a task for slaves, and Jews were even forbidden from asking Jewish slaves to do it. Yet this is the first time in the Gospels that Jesus talks about an "example" – and to this example, he ties a duty: "You must wash each other's feet." Is this only symbolic, when he goes on to say, "Do as I have done for you"?

Jean Vanier sees Jesus' injunction as more than symbolic. So, at the first L'Arche residence in Trosly, before the meal on Holy Thursday, they all washed each other's feet. Jean also did this at each of the retreats he held. He knows that when we put the gospel into *action*, instead of watching from a distance, this changes everything.

"Don't hide from your own flesh and blood who need your help."[47] This passage from the Book of Isaiah took on new meaning for Nadine Tokar, who founded the L'Arche community in Honduras. She was twenty-four years old when she visited several hospitals in Tegucigalpa, the Honduran capital. That day, she had entered a small room – little more than a closet – at the end of one of the hospital corridors. In a bed, caged in with wire mesh, there was a naked, wild child who bit her hand when she held it out. His name was Raphael. He was seven years old and severely disabled. He had been at the hospital since birth, and the nurses warned her to be careful. Nadine stayed at his side for a long time. "And then, all of a sudden, I felt a certainty," she recalls. "He couldn't stay there all his life. The sentence from Isaiah pierced me, truly pierced me: 'Don't hide from your flesh and blood who need your help.'"[48]

Nadine saw this little, broken child with twisted legs and arms that were too short as her own flesh. She welcomed Raphael into the L'Arche community in Tegucigalpa. They put up with his shouting, dirtying and breaking things, and biting those who came near him. He underwent an operation to improve the function of his legs. They accustomed him, little by little, to the sound of loving, caring human voices. And then, one day, as Nadine called to him, he looked her straight in the eyes and held out his hand to her.

In welcoming such a wounded child, in gathering around him to help him – because it takes more than one person – we have to

unite, to forget our divisions and differences. Jean Vanier has said
that the poor person is a unifier. If we cannot worship at the same
Eucharistic table, he writes in *The Broken Body*, we can at least
unite in our care for the poor. We can "welcome Jesus' invitation
to eat at the table of the poor and lame and disabled and blind. In
that way we will find God's special blessing." Eating together at
the same table, the table of the poor and weak, partaking of the
sacrament of the poor – "isn't this the most direct path to unity?"[49]

THE UNITY OF WHICH Jean Vanier often speaks – whether it
is unity within ourselves, the unity of Christians, or the unity of
society – does not suppress our sense of identity. On the contrary,
it grounds our individual identity in one we share with the
whole human race. "The awareness that we belong to a common
humanity, and that this belonging is more fundamental than any
other affiliation, has greatly changed my attitudes and my vision
of the human being. It has helped to free me from certain egocen-
tric behaviors and inner wounds and has incited me to care more
eagerly for those who are different, 'foreigners,' and even those
who attack us, our 'enemies.'"[50]

Unity does not erase differences. It is not a matter of uniformity,
but of finding the inner dynamism that lets all the parts work
together. Each person has an important role and contributes to
the functioning of the whole. The image that guides Jean Vanier's
thoughts, following Paul's famous comparison in the First Letter to
the Corinthians, is the image of the body made up of many parts.
He sees humanity as a body in which all the different parts are
useful. Jean Vanier finds in these words an allusion to people with
disabilities, for "those parts of the body that seem to be weaker are
indispensable."[51]

Paul also writes that the whole body suffers when one of
its members suffers, and the whole body rejoices if even one
of its members rejoices. For Jean Vanier, this means that we
must deconstruct our pyramid-shaped societies dominated by

a handful of powerful people at the top. We must deconstruct a world dominated by a few super-powerful nations, and follow the example of Christ, who humbled himself at the feet of his apostles. "It is the lowliest who transport us to the heights," Jean says.

We must take the opposite tack from the world, not trying to rise above those who are weak, but reaching down in order to meet them where they are. By doing this, paradoxically, we find ourselves. And by lifting them up, we lift ourselves along with them and thrive together. We cannot save ourselves by ourselves! This is not a question of doing good deeds, but of living a life in which each person, each part of the body, is indispensable. We would be horrified by our society, with its cult of force and power, with its millions of outcasts locked up in psychiatric hospitals, lying on sidewalks, or dying at our inhospitable borders, if only we saw it as God sees it: as a mutilated body. We are called to repair this broken body, Jean Vanier says, not by making great speeches or by dreaming of converting the whole world, but by reestablishing conditions of justice and creating places of peace – first of all in ourselves, then in our families, parishes, towns, and villages. It is possible to move from competition to cooperation, from rivalry to fellowship, from exclusion to acceptance. The gospel message is one of hope, and Jean Vanier is passing it on.

Golden Years in Trosly

IT HAS BEEN OVER FIFTY YEARS since Jean Vanier founded L'Arche, and he is still living in Trosly-Breuil, this village where he took up residence in 1964. Recently, he moved into a new house that is brighter and better equipped than the one where he lived for thirty years, after moving out of the L'Arche home. The house opens onto a small garden. A large window looks out onto the yard and a chapel that was once a barn. In his office, he has taped photos on a white board: Mother Teresa, Mahatma Gandhi, Etty Hillesum, Aung San Suu Kyi, his brother Benedict, Eric, and his mother.

There are also photos of those from L'Arche who have passed away: Raphaël Simi, Barbara Swanekamp, Claire de Miribel, and others. But it is the same man with the same smile who welcomes an uninterrupted flow of visitors with arms wide open.

Ever since this tall Canadian moved here, the little Picard village has welcomed visitors from all over the world. All kinds of languages are spoken in the streets of Trosly-Breuil, and at the train station in Compiègne the taxi drivers are familiar with Jean's address.

Although it still appears to be a sleepy little village, Trosly has changed quite a bit. The core group of villagers remains, but the population of assistants and people with disabilities has grown over the years. L'Arche now has ten houses, two of which are special care homes for adults with severe disabilities who need constant medical care. In addition, there are two occupational houses, a craft store, workshops where subcontracting jobs are performed, craft workshops, two cafeterias, and market gardens that provide work for one hundred and twenty workers with disabilities, along with thirty educators. A large hall named the Hosanna Room allows two hundred residents and guests to gather for celebrations.

It is no small feat to climb the Rue d'Orléans with Jean Vanier without being stopped dozens of times by passersby. There are many people to meet in the streets of Trosly. Clumsy people hobble along, hand in hand, while others travel in wheelchairs, their bodies broken or twisted. One hears confused words and sees contorted faces with blank expressions. But then, all of a sudden, there is a glowing smile, a hand held out in a hearty "Welcome!" or a warm "What's your name?" "They are so beautiful," says Jean Vanier. One meets lots of young people as well: Japanese, Canadian, English, Czech, Lebanese, Swedish, Iraqi, or French assistants. "They are beautiful too," I dare to say. "Oh, yes," he responds. "Their beauty is a reflection of those they care for."

A tranquil but vibrant atmosphere permeates the village. Little groups are engaged in discussion on doorsteps. People pass by; they call out to one another and greet one another. L'Arche members go from their homes to their workshops, to the church, to the cafeteria to have lunch, or to gather for a celebration. Indeed, there are many celebrations to organize in Trosly: many birthdays, sendoffs, and welcome parties. In addition to the members of L'Arche, there are pilgrims who come to attend retreats, rest, or meet Jean Vanier. There are officials, journalists, and television crews. There are religious sisters and brothers and seminarians who come for training courses. There are laypeople, some quite ordinary, others less so, like the homeless people and prostitutes invited to a retreat recently.

JEAN VANIER RETURNED to Trosly from Rome on March 25, 2014, after a face-to-face meeting with Pope Francis. When they met, they conversed and held hands for a long while. Jean Vanier thanked the pope for being a sign of the presence of Jesus in our world. He thanked him for encouraging the church to reach out to those on the fringes of society with great energy – and for having recently declared that they were the wounds on the crucified body of Christ. He thanked Francis for being the pope of tenderness.

Jean is sitting on a bench that runs along the outside wall of the church at Trosly. He appears massive next to a little person with a deformed body who is holding his hand and trying to get warm at his side. It is a spring evening and the grass is very green. Tables are being set for a snack. Community members are just leaving the church after Mass. There is a tall bouquet of lilies in front of the altar. Mass at Trosly: the scent of the lilies, the music, the songs, the silence. It is a silence so profound, so full, beneath the continuous swell of the sounds of suffering: the little cries, grunts, sighs, and cascades of laughter. A man, a child – he is ageless – eyes lifted heavenward, is clapping his hands, palm against palm, fingers stretched out, while laughing.

"So, how's the book coming along?" Fred, a former resident of Val Fleuri, is talking to me. "Do you remember? I'm the one who told you who Jean Vanier is. Do you remember?" Yes, I remember. You told me, "Jean, he's a happy man!" And you too, Fred, you seem to be happy. They all seem happy, there on the lawn on this spring evening. Laughter floats from the Rue d'Orléans as the assistants push the wheelchairs around in a little race.

"L'ARCHE IS TRULY a therapeutic place," says the psychiatrist Erol Franko. When I arrived in Trosly in 1967, there was a sort of mistrust, perhaps stemming from pricked consciences, on the part of professionals toward Jean Vanier's project. They thought he was some kind of dreamer. But then, they had to admit that many of the people he took in were improving. Not everyone did better in L'Arche: some had to return to the hospital, others found stability in more conventional care homes, and some were able to live independently and find work to support themselves.

Jean Vanier also says that L'Arche is a place of healing for the assistants. I think of Keiko, the assistant who took care of a woman named Hélène, and had come to the end of her rope. Hélène was like a block of stone. Although she was not blind or deaf, she didn't seem to see, hear, or feel anything. She did not react or show any emotion: not a sound, not a cry, not a sigh. Hélène reminded Jean of the children he had once seen in a Romanian orphanage, in beds behind bars, expressionless. There was no use shouting or calling out anymore if no one responded. Jean approached one of the little ones and took him in his arms, but the child threw himself violently backward, as if he had received an electric shock. "He was so scared," Jean remembers. "The child was so walled up in his despair, so distant from others that the least bit of contact hurt him."[52] Jean told Keiko to keep talking to Hélène "tenderly, to touch her gently, to hold her lovingly."[53] He added, "You will see, one day Hélène will smile at you." And one day, Hélène smiled.

So, what is Jean Vanier thinking about as he sits on the bench behind the little group drinking orange juice and eating cookies? Is he reflecting on his visit to Val Fleuri that Christmas in 1963, where he met people with intellectual disabilities for the first time? Is he thinking about the past, the work he has accomplished, of those who are gone, of the lectures he will give tomorrow to some young assistants?

Is he really who people say he is, or is he what he himself thinks he is? He loves a poem written by Dietrich Bonhoeffer. In 1944, while in prison in Berlin for resisting the Nazis, Bonhoeffer asked the question, "Who am I?" Quoting the poem, Jean Vanier also asks himself: Who am I?

Who am I?
These lonely questions
of mine mock me.
Whoever I am, You know.
O God, I am thine!

Epilogue

January 2019

THE STAGE IS LIT with images of the sea. Amid the noise of thundering waves, someone is swimming, swimming, swimming. She comes closer, crosses the ocean, and then retreats, zigzagging across the room, until she arrives on stage where there is a tall – really tall – young man who looks somewhat ill at ease. The swimmer starts telling a story. The young man stirs and begins to move. His face and movements are slightly hindered by a mental disability, but he mimes with heart. We recognize the story: that of a man born in Geneva on September 10, 1928, whose ninetieth birthday is being celebrated today.

On the screen behind the stage, we see the father and mother with a baby in a baptismal dress. We see a young child with his brothers and sister. Then, on stage, we see a young woman with Down syndrome in an evening dress. She is playing the part of Princess Margaret. A young naval officer dances clumsily, crushing her feet. The audience laughs and takes up the songs in chorus.

The young man learns to pray, then hesitates between the monastery and the priesthood. He earns a doctorate in philosophy and appears on the stage wearing a graduation gown. Then we witness his first encounter with Philippe and Raphaël and the beginnings of L'Arche and Faith and Light. L'Arche turns into an international movement: saris and boubous appear. The man abandons his suit and tie in favor of a blue jacket and a cap. He travels around the world, gives talks, meets popes, and visits communities. Time passes and the narrator's voice declares, "And now Jean is old." At L'Arche, they don't mince words. The audience applauds because their friend is still with them in spite of his age. On the stage, the young man who is playing Jean Vanier bends over his cane and shuffles in little steps toward an easy chair that is suddenly lit by a spotlight. Applause. Singing. And then Jean – "the real Jean," says the narrator – climbs onto the stage.

He, too, is bent over and walks with a cane. He also sits down carefully. He smiles. Then he begins to speak. He thanks the actors. He is delighted with the celebration that has brought together the community of Trosly-Breuil, members of the surrounding communities, and friends from near and far. "I never had a house," he says of his childhood. "We moved around a lot. My parents were diplomats, so we always lived in staff housing, but not in a house of our own. Not a home. I found my home here in Trosly-Breuil, in L'Arche. My house, my home, my family – they're all here." And then, after a great big cake is brought in, everyone begins to sing. Jean blows out the candles. It is just a simple family celebration.

FOUR AND A HALF YEARS have passed since we left Jean Vanier during that evening in March 2014, as the community regrouped on the green grass outside the church after Mass. That year of 2014 would be a full one for him.

There was, of course, the fiftieth anniversary of L'Arche. It was a huge, beautiful celebration of unity and "the tender hand of God who led us all," Jean wrote in the newsletter. In May, a meeting at Paray-le-Monial brought together two thousand people from different communities to celebrate, pray, and give thanks. In June, the communities spent time together and forged yet more intimate bonds across regions and countries.

The Paris festival celebrating L'Arche's fiftieth anniversary took place on September 27. To the surprise of the passersby, there was a gigantic parade of seven thousand people marching from the Hôtel de Ville to the Place de la République. The crowd shouted, sang, and danced in the streets as colorful balloons floated into the air. "What are you demonstrating against?" people asked. "Against nothing! We're celebrating! Come dance and eat cake with us." A huge cake was indeed awaiting their arrival at the Place de la République. Jean Vanier spoke about peace, while Philippe Pozzo di Borgo, a quadriplegic whose story is told in the film *The Untouchables*, spoke about silence and expectation. The singer Grégoire sang *"Allez, venez et entrez dans la danse"* (Let's get together and dance). So they danced on the Place de la République – marchers, wheelchairs, and pedestrians all mixed together.

In the beginning of October, a gathering at Trosly-Breuil brought together two people, a person with disabilities and an assistant, from each of the initial communities from every country of the world. Seventy people arrived from New Zealand, Australia, Japan, India, Africa, America, and Europe. Most had never been on an airplane or seen Paris before. Musa Kirokote, from Kenya, laughed a lot, amazed at this extravagant country he was discovering. It was a barren country, certainly quite poor, he recounted in a delightful little film,[1] where there was no grass, where the dogs wore clothes, and where there were no lions! The women are beautiful and kiss you, but the French don't know how to cook. They don't know how to make *ghiteri* or *ugali*, but they eat tree leaves, like goats, he said, as he poked at the salad on his plate with a dubious glance. Commenting on the taste of the snails – which he nonetheless ate – he said, "These poor people!"

On December 8, members of L'Arche gathered at the Elysée Palace to celebrate Jean-Pierre Crépieux, the fourth person with disabilities to be welcomed to Trosly. He was the first person with intellectual disabilities to receive the Legion of Honor, the highest order of merit in France. The president of France, François Hollande, decorated him in recognition of Jean-Pierre's contribution to the foundation of L'Arche and to society.

IN 2014 JEAN VANIER tasted fulfillment, but he also tasted mourning. In May, his brother Benedict died in Canada. Jean was able to be at his side, having asked him to hold on until he could arrive. "And that's what he did," Jean writes.

> I was at his bedside the day he died. He was lying there with his gentle, almost laughing smile, giving life to those near him even in his pain. He was a gentle and holy monk for sixty-eight years, seeking and radiating the presence of God. At one point he put his hand in my hand and there we rested and prayed together in silence, until his breathing and his heart stopped. I could not contain my tears; his doctor began to hand me Kleenex after Kleenex. I did not want to leave this peaceful place, this prayerful presence one to another, but of course I had to, for he had left this side of the river of visible life for the other side. The veil between the visible and the invisible is so thin, so slight. All his life he had been waiting for this moment, and for the meeting with the One he loved and for whom he had given all his life. He had gone to the other side. Thank you big brother! Now I must get on with life here.[2]

A month later, Jean's sister Thérèse fell in her room at the Little Sisters of the Poor in London. She was taken to the same hospital where she had been a doctor for many years, and where she had initiated palliative care for the dying. Jean was at her side, but she was agitated and "in a terrible agony" that no one could understand. He recalls:

> It was painful for me and others. Her cry of "please, please," was like a scream. Once back at the Little Sisters, she found peace. I spoke to the palliative care doctor who was looking after her there during her last moments when she seemed more or less unconscious. I asked him how long he thought she would live. He answered that she still had a spiritual work to be completed, a work of intercession. "She will leave when that work is completed." She died gently the next day.

Epilogue

Her funeral was so beautiful. A fitting and glorious fulfillment of the many years she had struggled and yearned for unity between churches. The funeral Mass, celebrated by Father David Stanley, took place in the Anglican Canterbury Cathedral with many, many of her friends and people from L'Arche. She was buried in the little cemetery of Barfreston, the village where she began the first community of L'Arche in the United Kingdom in 1974. She lies there at rest with the first people she had welcomed in the community. Thérèse was a wonderful woman, a magnificent woman, compassionate and kind, and such a competent doctor.

Now, Jean's older siblings are dead. Bernard, the one to whom he was the closest, was the first to die. All the relatives he has left now are a niece who lives a long way away and a younger brother, but they don't call each other very often. It is a time of mourning and loss.

Yet life, with its accompanying joys and challenges, continues. There are both sweet and difficult community moments, retreats to lead, prayer at Orval, silence, and contemplation of the swallows. There are health issues, concerns for this or that community, the illnesses of friends. Life, Jean Vanier's life, continues on the path that he chose a long time ago.

JEAN VANIER LIVES among the little people, but meets the great ones of this world. In December 2016, he was elevated to the rank of Commander of the Legion of Honor. Manuel Valls took pride in the fact that this ceremony and the reception following it was his last act in Matignon as prime minister. The atmosphere was both serious and easygoing: Jean Vanier only moves about with people from L'Arche homes, even in the gilded halls of palaces. "We are not in the National Assembly," said Manuel Valls, laughing along with the person with disabilities who punctuated each of his sentences like an echo. And Jean felt free to advise Valls to smile more when he appears on television.

In September 2017, Jean was invited to London by Queen Elizabeth, along with Celine and David of Val Fleuri, who had appeared in *Summer in the Forest*, Randall Wright's film about L'Arche. Jean had not seen the monarch since that trip when he was twenty years old, during his first military tour, but she welcomed him with his nickname, Jock. When I ask him what he thinks about these prestigious meetings, he remarks:

> I'm not that impressed with important people. I don't take myself too seriously and I don't take them too seriously. I manage to get into a deep, human relationship with them fairly quickly. What matters to me is that I keep spreading my message. It is not a question of doing good to the poor but of understanding that the poor, those who are different, do us good. This requires a real conversion.[3]

For several years now, Jean has broadened his vision of the poor from people with disabilities to all who are humiliated, rejected, or different. More and more, he has been happy to give retreats in Trosly for those who are on the margins of society: prostitutes, the homeless, homosexuals, or divorced and remarried people. He finds reason for hope in the birth of new communities such as the Association pour l'Amitié or the Lazare Association, which, a little like L'Arche, organize a common life between young professionals and people living on the streets.

Jean also advocates for a better understanding of Islam. He writes, "L'Arche has had the opportunity, from its origins, to become ecumenical and interreligious. This means that we must each deepen our own religious faith and find opportunities to meet our brothers and sisters from other churches or religions. The essential thing for each of us is to let God live more and more in us, to see in each person the child of God."

Jean has been impressed, too, by the work of Nayla Tabbara and Father Fadi Daou, the Muslim woman and the Christian man who founded the Adyan Foundation, an interfaith training center in

Beirut that promotes understanding between Lebanese Christians and Muslims. After Jean met with them, they also began helping Muslim members of Faith and Light and L'Arche to deepen the spirituality of their communities. Nayla and Father Fadi came to Trosly to lead retreats on "divine hospitality in the Christian and Muslim vision." And Jean Vanier received the 2018 Adyan Prize on behalf of L'Arche.

Jean's dedication to achieving unity through our common humanity continues. He speaks with emotion of two women – one an Israeli whose son was killed by a Palestinian, the other a Palestinian whose son was killed by Israeli soldiers. After many difficulties, they were able to meet each other and discover their common humanity. "Their common suffering created a friendship that transcends the walls of separation, hostility, revenge, and hatred."[4] Together they wrote *Nos larmes ont la même couleur* (Our tears are the same color).

It is high time, says Jean Vanier, to get to know one another better and to make peace with one another if we do not want the world to sink into the fear and hatred that terrorism strives to arouse everywhere. "Humanity seems to have lost the path to life," he wrote at Christmas 2015, upon his return from the L'Arche community in Bethlehem, Ma'an lil-Hayat (Together for Life), his last official trip to a community. "Yet I would like this letter, far from being a cry of sadness, discouragement, or weakness, to be a small sign of hope in the face of all the difficulties, insecurities, and fears that can overwhelm us. Personally, I felt the [Paris terror attacks] of November 13 were a call, in the face of the savagery of these young jihadists. I do not want to sink into fear, discouragement, and even hatred; I want rather to get up and become a peacemaker myself, living my faith in Jesus who is our peace." Jean makes similar remarks in his recent book *A Cry Is Heard: My Path to Peace*,[5] in which he applies his personal journey and the spirituality of L'Arche to reflections on the evolution of humanity and the future of the world.

YET ANOTHER ORDEAL was awaiting Jean. Just one month after his eighty-ninth birthday, on October 13, 2017, he had a heart attack at his home in Trosly. The ambulance took him away, sirens screaming, to the hospital in Compiègne. He went into surgery. Then he went to rest by the sea. "This heart attack was a sign to me," he says. "I always thought there would be a sign and that, at that sign, I would stop what I was doing. Of course the doctors asked me to rest, but I made the decision. It is the beginning of a whole new life: no more trips, retreats, or conferences."[6]

It seems that giving up retreats and talks has not been difficult for him. He does, however, miss talking to assistants in training sessions.

> One of the things I still do are little four-and-a-half minute videos where I continue to relate what I learned at L'Arche, this message that is very dear to my heart, this mystery that is so important to me – that the lowest of people can transform us if we are willing to meet them, to come in contact with them. And this encounter requires a lot of humility. Don't tell people what to do, but love them. Listen to their cry. "Do you love me?" is the cry of the poor; it's the wisdom of the poor.

Jean continues to reflect, too, on the life of the church:

> It seems to me that today there are two conceptions of the church: that of a church that must be very stable with a clear doctrine, a reassuring church, and on the other hand a more open church, a church of relationships.
>
> I feel very close to Pope Francis. I feel a kind of harmony between what he says and what I think: that you have to go to the outskirts and meet people and discover their wisdom. I am touched when I see him go to the places where people are most damaged: prisons, hospitals, slums. Francis is concerned that the church should go out to reach the poor. It is not a question of building a citadel. And, of course, all this can make us vulnerable.

Since his heart attack, Jean has been spending the mornings by himself in his room, resting and, above all, taking "a time of union with Jesus." He prays, reads the Bible, and reads a book: one by theologian José Antonio Pagola, *Jesus: An Historical Approximation*, another by black American pastor Howard Thurman, *Jesus and the Disinherited*. He is happy in this silence, and acknowledges that this solitude suits the somewhat solitary side of his personality. He has always had a taste for prayer and scriptural meditation, as in the days when he lived alone, a little like a hermit, in Normandy and then in Fatima.

Jean only eats lunch out once a week. Otherwise, the Farm brings him his meals, which he sometimes shares with a guest or two. Wisely, he naps each day. He also walks, as the doctor has advised, for thirty to forty minutes daily. But he doesn't leave his premises. In Trosly, the sidewalks are narrow and the streets are full of acquaintances, so he walks up the alley in front of his house in one direction, then in the other, as he did on the ship's deck when he was sailing. He meets with people who want to see him – people from the various L'Arche communities, as well as others, some unknown, some important. Brigitte Macron, the wife of French President Emmanuel Macron, came once. The afternoon passes quickly. At 6 p.m. he goes to the chapel for Mass. Then, after dinner, he meditates in the oratory or at home.

Jean feels surrounded, pampered even, by his community. He recounts with emotion how a woman he took in years ago declared one evening with tenderness: "At first we needed Jean, now Jean needs us."

Yes, he needs others. He's more fragile. He tires quickly. He can't see or hear as well. Walking is less easy and less fluid. He needs help getting up from his chair. All these losses, these limitations that old age inevitably brings, he seems to welcome in peace and gentleness, as he would welcome long-awaited friends. When I ask him about his age, there is even a bit of amusement in his tone: his blue eyes sparkle and he smiles.

What will I be in a year, two years from now? It is obvious that I will move towards greater fragility. For the moment I have my mind, but there will come a time when I will lose my memory, perhaps my mobility. How can one be reconciled to that?

Today, I realize that I no longer have a future. Most of the people I see have a future and that future is linked to a reputation, a project, a desire: to become a better journalist, a better doctor, or a better parent. They strive to be better. For me, it's not that at all; it's about living in the present moment and making that moment a place where the important thing is to be open to what the other brings me.

I am happy. Many older people feel lonely. I am not alone. I am in a community where I feel loved. A few days ago, there was a meeting here with the new community leaders. They came from the Philippines, Cairo, and elsewhere. I came by to say hello. There was a kind of love, excitement, and joy to meet me, even though I barely stayed with them for fifteen minutes. There was a joy in meeting the old grandfather but also the founder.

Jean is lucid and peaceful, serious but joyful, on this sunny day in early October when we talk in his office. He continues:

The other day I wondered what would happen if I couldn't walk anymore. I did have a little pinch in my heart at the thought. But at the present moment, I'm happy. L'Arche is in good hands. Wonderful people are taking care of it. I have no more responsibilities there at all. I see Christine McGrievy, the director of the Trosly community, regularly but it's because she cares about me. She wants to make sure I'm okay. Odile Ceyrac takes care of me admirably, especially the whole medical aspect.[7]

It wasn't his legs that weakened first, but his voice. At the end of October 2018, Jean began to have trouble speaking. In December he underwent an operation and was found to have thyroid cancer. Mid-January, he began radiation therapy. The disease is expanding its grip. Shortly after his ninetieth birthday he wrote:

Epilogue

I know that new weaknesses, new forms of poverty and new losses are waiting for me. It will be the descent into what is essential, that which is most hidden in me, deeper than all the parts of success and shadow inside me. That will be what is left when all the rest is gone. My naked person, a primal innocence which is awaiting its encounter with God.[8]

Jean Vanier died on May 7, 2019, as this book was going to press.

Acknowledgements

FIRST OF ALL, I wish to thank Jean Vanier, who agreed to receive me as often as I wished for long interviews and generously opened his personal archives and documentation for me. Thank you, as well, to all who spoke with me about Jean Vanier, L'Arche, and Faith and Light, both in interviews and during informal encounters. Special thanks go to Odile Ceyrac, Gérard Daucourt, Erol Franko, Frédéric Guillemet, Françoise Laroudie, Marie-Hélène Mathieu, Stephan Posner, Alain Saint Macary, and Nadine Tokar. Thanks also to the many people I have not specifically named whose remarks, stories, and perspectives on L'Arche and its founder have rounded out this portrait. Furthermore, 1 wish to thank all the disabled people, assistants, and friends of L'Arche and Faith and Light who, over the past twenty-five years, have welcomed me as a friend into their households and communities. And finally, thanks to Isabelle Aumont, director of the Association Jean Vanier, for the photographic documentation.

Anne-Sophie Constant

Notes

Introduction

1. Jean Vanier, *L'histoire de l'Arche* (Ottawa: Novalis, 1995), 21.

Child of War

1. Julia Kristeva and Jean Vanier, *Leur regard perce nos ombres* (Paris: Fayard, 2011), 58.
2. Jean Vanier, *Ma faiblesse, c'est ma force* (Montreal: Bellarmin, 1975), 45.
3. Jean Vanier, *Ma faiblesse, c'est ma force*, 44.
4. Jacques Tremblay, "Le général Vanier donner et se donner," *Adsum*, August 14, 2013.
5. Jean Vanier, *Ma faiblesse, c'est ma force*, 34.
6. Interview with Jean Vanier, September 17, 2013.
7. Jean Vanier, *Aimer jusqu'au bout* (Toronto: Novalis, 1996), 48.
8. Or more precisely, "Envoy Extraordinary and Minister Plenipotentiary to France," since the Canadian legation to France did not yet have the rank of ambassador.
9. Jean Vanier, "*Conférence aux prêtres de Rome,*" November 2012.
10. Interview with Jean Vanier, September 17, 2013.
11. Major-Général Georges Philias Vanier, *Paroles de guerre* (Montreal: Beauchemin, 1944), 47, 56, 138.
12. Interview with Jean Vanier, September 17, 2013.
13. Interview with Jean Vanier, September 17, 2013.
14. Interview with Jean Vanier, September 17, 2013.
15. Interview with Jean Vanier, November 22, 2013.
16. Jean Vanier, *Une porte d'espérance* (Paris: Éditions de l'Atelier, 1993), 14.
17. Mary Frances Coady, *Georges and Pauline Vanier: Portrait of a Couple* (Montreal: McGill-Queen's University Press, 2011), 177.

Officer

1. Kristeva and Vanier, *Leur regard perce nos ombres*, 56.
2. Interview with Jean Vanier, November 22, 2013.
3. Interview with Jean Vanier, November 22, 2013.
4. Jean Vanier, *Homme et femme, Dieu les fit* (Paris: Presses de la Renaissance, 2009), 160.
5. Kristeva and Vanier, *Leur regard perce nos ombres*, 48.
6. Interview with Jean Vanier, November 22, 2013.
7. Interview with Jean Vanier, November 22, 2013.

8. René Girard, *Discours à l'Académie française, Éloge du père Carré*, December 15, 2005.

9. Isa. 43:4

10. Jean Vanier, *La source des larmes* (Paris: Parole et Silence, 2001), 42, 59.

11. Thomas Merton, *The Seven Storey Mountain* (New York: Harcourt, Brace & Company, 1948), 340.

12. Merton, *The Seven Storey Mountain*, 342–3.

13. Interview with Jean Vanier, November 22, 2013.

14. Quoted by Kathryn Spink, *Jean Vanier et l'aventure de l'Arche* (Montreal: Novalis, 2007), 37.

Disciple

1. Jean Vanier, *Drawn into the Mystery of Jesus through the Gospel of John* (New York: Paulist Press, 2004), 39.

2. Gen. 12:1–2

3. Interview with Jean Vanier, September 17, 2013.

4. Saint Teresa of Avila, *The Life of St. Teresa of Jesus, of the Order of Our Lady of Carmel* (New York: Columbus Press, 1911), 123.

5. Interview with Jean Vanier, September 22, 2013.

6. Jean Vanier, *Ma faiblesse, c'est ma force*, 19.

7. Saint François de Sales, *Lettres intimes* (Paris: Sarment Fayard, 1991), 97.

8. Interview with Jean Vanier, November 22, 2013.

9. Dietrich Bonhoeffer, Protestant German pastor, radical opponent of Nazism since 1935, was imprisoned in 1943, then deported to Buchenwald and hung in the Flossenbürg camp in 1945.

10. Interview with Jean Vanier, December 20, 2013.

11. Interview with Jean Vanier, December 20, 2013.

Founder

1. Jean Vanier, *L'histoire de l'Arche*, 11.

2. Interview with Jean Vanier, December 20, 2013.

3. Interview with Jean Vanier, December 20, 2013.

4. Jean Vanier, *Une porte d'espérance*, 17.

5. Jean Vanier, *L'histoire de l'Arche*, 16.

6. *Lettres de L'Arche*, No. 8.

7. Jean Vanier, *Notre vie ensemble* (Paris: Médiaspaul, 2009), 29.

8. Jean Vanier, *Notre vie ensemble*, 30.

9. Interview with Jean Vanier, July 1, 2013.

10. Jean Vanier, *The Heart of L'Arche: A Spirituality for Every Day* (London: SPCK, 2013), 68.

11. Antoinette Maurice, *Cette richesse qui vient du pauvre*, internal

document at L'Arche, 2007, 28.

12. Maurice, *Cette richesse qui vient du pauvre*, 29.
13. Interview with Alain Saint Macary, October 17, 2013.
14. Interview with Odile Ceyrac, October 18, 2013.
15. Jean Vanier, *The Heart of L'Arche*, 67.
16 Madame Weltkij, quoted in Maurice, *Cette richesse qui vient du pauvre*, 78.
17. Jean Vanier, *L'histoire de l'Arche*, 20.
18. Jean Vanier, *L'histoire de l'Arche*, 19.
19. This book was written and published in France before these allegations came to light. The author has added this section for this English edition. —Ed.
20. Jean Vanier, Letter to the International Leadership Team, October 17, 2016.
21. Interview with Jean Vanier, September 17, 2013.
22. Matt. 13:31–32
23. Jean Vanier, *L'histoire de l'Arche*, 32.

Guide

1. Jean Vanier, *Ma faiblesse, c'est ma force*, 15.
2. Interview with Françoise Laroudie, January 16, 2014.
3. Martha Bala, *"Une présence hors du commun,"* www.jean-vanier.org.
4. Interview with Jean Vanier, March 14, 2014.
5. 1 Kings 3:9
6. John 8:31–32 (MEV)
7. Jean Vanier, *Notre vie ensemble*, 220.
8. Interview with Jean Vanier, July 1, 2013.
9. Jean Vanier, *Notre vie ensemble*, 28.
10. Matt. 13:35
11. Jean Vanier, *Drawn into the Mystery of Jesus through the Gospel of John*, 161.
12. Jean Vanier, *Drawn into the Mystery of Jesus through the Gospel of John*, 166.
13. Mark 10:29–30

Pilgrim

1. Interview with Alain Saint Macary, October 17, 2013.
2. Jean Vanier, *L'histoire de l'Arche*, 74.
3. Jean Vanier, *Une porte d'espérance*, 89.
4. Jean Vanier, *"Le pauvre, chemin d'unité,"* opening speech for the Conseil oecuménique des Églises, Canada, 1983.

5. Jean Vanier, *Notre vie ensemble*, 13.

6. Marie-Hélène Mathieu with Jean Vanier, *Plus jamais seuls, l'aventure foi et lumière* (Paris: Presses de la Renaissance, 2011), 29.

7. René Leroy, *Moi, tout seul, pas capable* (Paris: Le Livre Ouvert, 2004), 29.

8. Interview with Jean Vanier, February 19, 2014.

9. 1 Cor. 12:22–23

10. Interview with Jean Vanier, Lourdes, 1971 (DVD).

11. "Les communautés Faith and Light," *Ombres et Lumière*, December 1978, 6.

12. Jean Vanier, *Notre vie ensemble*, 57.

13. UNAEDE, Union nationale des assistants et des éducateurs de l'enfance (National Union of Childhood Assistants and Educators).

14. Mathieu, *Plus jamais seuls*, 79.

15. Le Secrétariat catholique de l'enfance et de la jeunesse inadaptées (Catholic secretariat for children and youth with disabilities).

16. Interview with Jean Vanier, Lourdes, 1971 (DVD).

17. Interview with Jean Vanier, Lourdes, 1971 (DVD).

18. Mathieu, *Plus jamais seuls*, 129.

19. Mathieu, *Plus jamais seuls*, 159.

20. Mathieu, *Plus jamais seuls*, 155.

21. Mathieu, *Plus jamais seuls*, 193.

22. Jean Vanier, *Toute personne est une histoire sacrée* (Paris: Plon, 1994), 180.

23. Interview with Stephan Posner, January 23, 2014.

24. Jean Vanier, *Toute personne est une histoire sacrée*, 132.

25. Jean Vanier, *Toute personne est une histoire sacrée*, 133.

26. Kristeva and Vanier, *Leur regard perce nos ombres*, 233.

27. Eléna Lasida, *Évaluer l'utilité sociale de l'Arche*, internal document, 9.

28. Interview with Jean Vanier, February 9, 2014.

29. Jean Vanier, *Notre vie ensemble*, 221.

Messenger

1. Isa. 52:7

2. Interview with Gérard Daucourt, October 23, 2013.

3. Interview with Jean Vanier, July 1, 2013.

4. Interview with Stephan Posner, January 23, 2014.

5. Jacques Dufresne, *"Jean Vanier: de l'admiration convenue à la compréhension assumée,"* www.appartenance-belonging.org.

6. Jer. 17:9

7. Interview with Jean Vanier, September 17, 2013.

8. Exod. 24:7. The word "understand" is generally translated differently in English. It also means to listen or to obey.

9. Matt. 5:38–39

10. Blaise Pascal, *Of the Geometric Spirit,* part 2, "The Art of Persuasion."

11. Jean Vanier, *Les signes des temps: à la lumière de Vatican II* (Paris: Albin Michel, 2012), 145.

12. 1 John 1:1

13. Matt. 11:25

14. 1 Cor. 1:27–28

15. Jean Vanier, *Accueillir notre humanité* (Paris: Presses de la Renaissance, 1999), 12.

16. Jean Vanier, *Une porte d'espérance,* 19.

17. Jean Vanier, *Toute personne est une histoire sacrée,* 56.

18. Jean Vanier, keynote address to the priests of the diocese of Rome, 2012.

19. *The Broken Body* is the title of one of Jean Vanier's books.

20. 1 Cor. 6:19

21. Jean Vanier, *Jésus, le don de l'amour* (Paris: Fleurus, 1994).

22. Vanier, *Toute personne est une histoire sacrée,* 60.

23. Interview with Jean Vanier, January 24, 2014.

24. Interview with Jean Vanier, January 24, 2014.

25. Pierre Emmanuel, *"Le livre de l'homme et de la femme," Oeuvres poétiques complètes,* II (Lausanne: L'Âge d'homme, 2004), 974.

26. Luke 9:48

27. Jean Vanier, *Le Seigneur te guidera constamment* (Trosly-Breuil, France: Les Chemins de l'Arche–La Ferme, 1988), 17.

28. Luke 11:28

29. Luke 14:15

30. Luke 12:36–37

31. John 20:29

32. John 13:12–17

33. Kristeva and Vanier, *Leur regard perce nos ombres,* 23.

34. Jean Vanier, *La communauté, lieu du pardon et de la fête* (Paris: Fleurus, 1979, 1989).

35. John 15:11

36. Hos. 2:15

37. Message from Pope John Paul II to the participants of the international symposium on the theme of the dignity and rights of mentally disabled people, January 5, 2004.

38. Jean Vanier, *Notre vie ensemble,* 620.

39. Jean Vanier, *Accueillir notre humanité,* 161.

40. Interview with Nadine Tokar, January 24, 2014.

41. Speech delivered on January 29, 2014 at UNESCO.
42. Interview with Odile Ceyrac, October 18, 2013.
43. Interview with Jean Vanier, January 24, 2014.
44. Albert Jacquard, *Le souci des pauvres* (Montreal: Flammarion, 1996).
45. Jean Vanier, *La communauté, lieu du pardon et de la fête*, 313.
46. John 13:1–17
47. Isa. 58:7 (TLB)
48. Interview with Nadine Tokar, January 24, 2014.
49. Jean Vanier, *Le corps brisé: Retour vers la communion* (Montreal: Bellarmin, 1989), 141.
50. Jean Vanier, *Accueillir notre humanité*, 10.
51. Cor. 12:12–13
52. Jean Vanier, *La source des larmes*, 136.
53. Jean Vanier, *La source des larmes*, 136.

Epilogue

1. *As I am*, L'Arche International, www.larche.org.
2. Jean Vanier's Letter, September 2014.
3. Interview with Jean Vanier, October 10, 2018.
4. Jean Vanier's Letter, November 2016.
5. Jean Vanier and François Xavier Maigre, *A Cry Is Heard: My Path to Peace* (New London, CT: Twenty-Third Publications, 2018).
6. Interview with Jean Vanier, October 10, 2018.
7. Interview with Jean Vanier, October 10, 2018.
8. Jean Vanier's Letter, October 2018.

Selected Bibliography

Works by Jean Vanier

Accueillir notre humanité. Paris: Presses de la Renaissance, 1999. *(Becoming Human)*

Aimer jusqu'au bout. Toronto: Novalis, 1996. *(The Scandal of Service)*

Entrer dans le mystère de Jésus. Une lecture de l'Évangile de Jean. Paris: Novalis-Bayard, 2005. *(Drawn into the Mystery of Jesus through the Gospel of John)*

Homme et femme, Dieu les fit. Paris: Presses de la Renaissance, 2009. *(Man and Woman God Made Them)*

Jésus, le don de l'amour. Paris: Fleurus, 1994. *(Jesus, the Gift of Love)*

L'histoire de l'Arche. Ottawa: Novalis, 1995. *(An Ark for the Poor)*

La communauté, lieu du pardon et de la fête. Paris: Fleurus, 1979. *(Community and Growth)*

La source des larmes. Paris: Parole et Silence, 2001. *(Befriending the Stranger)*

Le corps brisé: Retour vers la communion. Montreal: Bellarmin, 1989. *(The Broken Body)*

Le Seigneur te guidera constamment. Trosly-Breuil, France: Les Chemins de l'Arche–La Ferme, 1988.

Les signes des temps: à la lumière de Vatican II. Paris: Albin Michel, 2012. *(Signs of the Times)*

Ma faiblesse, c'est ma forcé. Montreal: Bellarmin, 1975. *(In Weakness, Strength)*

Notre vie ensemble. Paris: Médiaspaul, 2009. *(Our Life Together)*

La spiritualité de l'Arche. Ottawa: Novalis, 1995. *(The Heart of L'Arche)*

Toute personne est une histoire sacrée. Paris: Plon, 1994.

Une porte d'espérance. Paris: Éditions de l'Atelier, 1993. *(A Door of Hope)*

In Collaboration

Kristeva, Julia, and Jean Vanier. *Leur regard perce nos ombres.* Paris: Fayard, 2011.

Mathieu, Marie-Hélène, with Jean Vanier. *Plus jamais seuls, l'aventure foi et lumière.* Paris: Presses de la Renaissance, 2011. *(Never Again Alone)*

Vanier, Jean, and François Xavier Maigre. *A Cry Is Heard: My Path to Peace.* New London, CT: Twenty-Third Publications, 2018.

Other Works

Coady, Mary Frances. *Georges and Pauline Vanier: Portrait of a Couple.* Montreal: McGill-Queen's University, 2011.

Emmanuel, Pierre. *"Le livre de l'homme et de la femme," Oeuvres poétiques complètes, II.* Lausanne: L'Âge d'homme, 2004.

François de Sales. *Lettres intimes.* Paris: Sarment Fayard, 1991.

Girard, René. *Discours à l'Académie française, Éloge du père Carré.* December 15, 2005.

Jacquard, Albert. *Le souci des pauvres.* Montreal: Flammarion, 1996.

Leroy, René. *Moi, tout seul, pas capable.* Paris: Le Livre Ouvert, 2004.

Maurice, Antoinette. *Cette richesse qui vient du pauvre.* 2007.

Merton, Thomas. *The Seven Storey Mountain.* New York: Harcourt, Brace, 1948.

Pascal, Blaise. *Of the Geometric Spirit*, part 2, "The Art of Persuasion."

Spink, Kathryn. *Jean Vanier et l'aventure de l'Arche.* Montreal: Novalis, 2007.

Teresa of Avila. *The Life of St. Teresa of Jesus, of the Order of Our Lady of Carmel.* New York: Columbus, 1911.

Vanier, Major-Général Georges Philias. *Paroles de guerre.* Montreal: Beauchemin, 1944.

Other Titles from Plough

The Reckless Way of Love
Notes on Following Jesus
Dorothy Day

Homage to a Broken Man
The Life of J. Heinrich Arnold – A true story of faith, forgiveness, sacrifice, and community
Peter Mommsen

Called to Community
The Life Jesus Wants for His People
Charles Moore, editor

Why We Live in Community
with two interpretive talks by Thomas Merton
Eberhard Arnold

Stronger than Death
How Annalena Tonelli Defied Death, Terror, and Tuberculosis in the Horn of Africa
Rachel Pieh Jones

Plough Publishing House
PO BOX 398, Walden, NY 12586, USA
Robertsbridge, East Sussex TN32 5DR, UK
4188 Gwydir Highway, Elsmore, NSW 2360, Australia
845-572-3455 • info@plough.com
www.plough.com